*Mobility of Capital in the Ca* [...]
*Economic Union*

# Mobility of Capital in the Canadian Economic Union

Nicolas Roy

*Published by the University of Toronto Press in cooperation with the Royal Commission on the Economic Union and Development Prospects for Canada and the Canadian Government Publishing Centre, Supply and Services Canada*

University of Toronto Press
*Toronto      Buffalo      London*

©Minister of Supply and Services Canada 1986

Printed in Canada
ISBN 0-8020-7313-1
ISSN 0829-2396
Cat. No. Z1-1983/1-41-66E

CANADIAN CATALOGUING IN PUBLICATION DATA

Roy, Nicolas, 1956–
  Mobility of capital in the Canadian economic union

(The Collected research studies / Royal Commission on the Economic Union and Development Prospects for Canada,
ISSN 0829-2396 ; 66)
Includes bibliographical references.
ISBN 0-8020-7313-1

1. Capital movements — Law and legislation — Canada. 2. Capital movements — Canada. 3. Canada — Economic policy. 4. Federal–provincial fiscal relations — Canada. I. Royal Commission on the Economic Union and Development Prospects for Canada. II. Title. III. Series: The Collected research studies (Royal Commission on the Economic Union and Development Prospects for Canada) ; 66.

KE1408.R69 1985      346.71'07      C85-099657-0

PUBLISHING COORDINATION: Ampersand Communications Services Inc.
COVER DESIGN: Will Rueter
INTERIOR DESIGN: Brant Cowie/Artplus Limited

# CONTENTS

# FOREWORD

When the members of the Rowell-Sirois Commission began their collective task in 1937, very little was known about the evolution of the Canadian economy. What was known, moreover, had not been extensively analyzed by the slender cadre of social scientists of the day.

When we set out upon our task nearly 50 years later, we enjoyed a substantial advantage over our predecessors; we had a wealth of information. We inherited the work of scholars at universities across Canada and we had the benefit of the work of experts from private research institutes and publicly sponsored organizations such as the Ontario Economic Council and the Economic Council of Canada. Although there were still important gaps, our problem was not a shortage of information; it was to interrelate and integrate — to synthesize — the results of much of the information we already had.

The mandate of this Commission is unusually broad. It encompasses many of the fundamental policy issues expected to confront the people of Canada and their governments for the next several decades. The nature of the mandate also identified, in advance, the subject matter for much of the research and suggested the scope of enquiry and the need for vigorous efforts to interrelate and integrate the research disciplines. The resulting research program, therefore, is particularly noteworthy in three respects: along with original research studies, it includes survey papers which synthesize work already done in specialized fields; it avoids duplication of work which, in the judgment of the Canadian research community, has already been well done; and, considered as a whole, it is the most thorough examination of the Canadian economic, political and legal systems ever undertaken by an independent agency.

The Commission's research program was carried out under the joint direction of three prominent and highly respected Canadian scholars: Dr. Ivan Bernier (*Law and Constitutional Issues*), Dr. Alan Cairns (*Politics and Institutions of Government*) and Dr. David C. Smith (*Economics*).

Dr. Ivan Bernier is Dean of the Faculty of Law at Laval University. Dr. Alan Cairns is former Head of the Department of Political Science at the University of British Columbia and, prior to joining the Commission, was William Lyon Mackenzie King Visiting Professor of Canadian Studies at Harvard University. Dr. David C. Smith, former Head of the Department of Economics at Queen's University in Kingston, is now Principal of that University. When Dr. Smith assumed his new responsibilities at Queen's in September 1984, he was succeeded by Dr. Kenneth Norrie of the University of Alberta and John Sargent of the federal Department of Finance, who together acted as Co-directors of Research for the concluding phase of the Economics research program.

I am confident that the efforts of the Research Directors, research coordinators and authors whose work appears in this and other volumes, have provided the community of Canadian scholars and policy makers with a series of publications that will continue to be of value for many years to come. And I hope that the value of the research program to Canadian scholarship will be enhanced by the fact that Commission research is being made available to interested readers in both English and French.

I extend my personal thanks, and that of my fellow Commissioners, to the Research Directors and those immediately associated with them in the Commission's research program. I also want to thank the members of the many research advisory groups whose counsel contributed so substantially to this undertaking.

DONALD S. MACDONALD

At its most general level, the Royal Commission's research program has examined how the Canadian political economy can better adapt to change. As a basis of enquiry, this question reflects our belief that the future will always take us partly by surprise. Our political, legal and economic institutions should therefore be flexible enough to accommodate surprises and yet solid enough to ensure that they help us meet our future goals. This theme of an adaptive political economy led us to explore the interdependencies between political, legal and economic systems and drew our research efforts in an interdisciplinary direction.

The sheer magnitude of the research output (more than 280 separate studies in 70+ volumes) as well as its disciplinary and ideological diversity have, however, made complete integration impossible and, we have concluded, undesirable. The research output as a whole brings varying perspectives and methodologies to the study of common problems and we therefore urge readers to look beyond their particular field of interest and to explore topics across disciplines.

The three research areas, — *Law and Constitutional Issues*, under Ivan Bernier; *Politics and Institutions of Government*, under Alan Cairns; and *Economics*, under David C. Smith (co-directed with Kenneth Norrie and John Sargent for the concluding phase of the research program) — were further divided into 19 sections headed by research coordinators.

The area *Law and Constitutional Issues* has been organized into five major sections headed by the research coordinators identified below.

- Law, Society and the Economy — *Ivan Bernier and Andrée Lajoie*
- The International Legal Environment — *John J. Quinn*
- The Canadian Economic Union — *Mark Krasnick*

- Harmonization of Laws in Canada — *Ronald C.C. Cuming*
- Institutional and Constitutional Arrangements — *Clare F. Beckton and A. Wayne MacKay*

Since law in its numerous manifestations is the most fundamental means of implementing state policy, it was necessary to investigate how and when law could be mobilized most effectively to address the problems raised by the Commission's mandate. Adopting a broad perspective, researchers examined Canada's legal system from the standpoint of how law evolves as a result of social, economic and political changes and how, in turn, law brings about changes in our social, economic and political conduct.

Within *Politics and Institutions of Government*, research has been organized into seven major sections.

- Canada and the International Political Economy — *Denis Stairs and Gilbert Winham*
- State and Society in the Modern Era — *Keith Banting*
- Constitutionalism, Citizenship and Society — *Alan Cairns and Cynthia Williams*
- The Politics of Canadian Federalism — *Richard Simeon*
- Representative Institutions — *Peter Aucoin*
- The Politics of Economic Policy — *G. Bruce Doern*
- Industrial Policy — *André Blais*

This area examines a number of developments which have led Canadians to question their ability to govern themselves wisely and effectively. Many of these developments are not unique to Canada and a number of comparative studies canvass and assess how others have coped with similar problems. Within the context of the Canadian heritage of parliamentary government, federalism, a mixed economy, and a bilingual and multicultural society, the research also explores ways of rearranging the relationships of power and influence among institutions to restore and enhance the fundamental democratic principles of representativeness, responsiveness and accountability.

*Economics* research was organized into seven major sections.

- Macroeconomics — *John Sargent*
- Federalism and the Economic Union — *Kenneth Norrie*
- Industrial Structure — *Donald G. McFetridge*
- International Trade — *John Whalley*
- Income Distribution and Economic Security — *François Vaillancourt*
- Labour Markets and Labour Relations — *Craig Riddell*
- Economic Ideas and Social Issues — *David Laidler*

Economics research examines the allocation of Canada's human and other resources, the ways in which institutions and policies affect this allocation, and the distribution of the gains from their use. It also considers the nature of economic development, the forces that shape our regional and industrial structure, and our economic interdependence with other countries. The thrust of the research in economics is to increase our comprehension of what determines our economic potential and how instruments of economic policy may move us closer to our future goals.

One section from each of the three research areas — The Canadian Economic Union, The Politics of Canadian Federalism, and Federalism and the Economic Union — have been blended into one unified research effort. Consequently, the volumes on Federalism and the Economic Union as well as the volume on The North are the results of an inter-disciplinary research effort.

We owe a special debt to the research coordinators. Not only did they organize, assemble and analyze the many research studies and combine their major findings in overviews, but they also made substantial contributions to the Final Report. We wish to thank them for their performance, often under heavy pressure.

Unfortunately, space does not permit us to thank all members of the Commission staff individually. However, we are particularly grateful to the Chairman, The Hon. Donald S. Macdonald; the Commission's Executive Director, J. Gerald Godsoe; and the Director of Policy, Alan Nymark, all of whom were closely involved with the Research Program and played key roles in the contribution of Research to the Final Report. We wish to express our appreciation to the Commission's Administrative Advisor, Harry Stewart, for his guidance and advice, and to the Director of Publishing, Ed Matheson, who managed the research publication process. A special thanks to Jamie Benidickson, Policy Coordinator and Special Assistant to the Chairman, who played a valuable liaison role between Research and the Chairman and Commissioners. We are also grateful to our office administrator, Donna Stebbing, and to our secretarial staff, Monique Carpentier, Barbara Cowtan, Tina DeLuca, Françoise Guilbault and Marilyn Sheldon.

Finally, a well deserved thank you to our closest assistants: Jacques J.M. Shore, *Law and Constitutional Issues*; Cynthia Williams and her successor Karen Jackson, *Politics and Institutions of Government*; and I. Lilla Connidis, *Economics*. We appreciate not only their individual contribution to each research area, but also their cooperative contribution to the research program and the Commission.

IVAN BERNIER
ALAN CAIRNS
DAVID C. SMITH

This monograph is the second of four volumes exploring the operation of the Canadian economic union. In studying economic unions, many writers have followed the progression first formulated by Bela Balassa, who has written that "from its lowest to highest forms, integration has been said to progress through the freeing of barriers to trade, the liberalization of factor movement, the harmonization of national economic policies and the total unification of these policies."

The first volume in this series, *Perspectives on the Canadian Economic Union* (Volume 60), looks at trade integration and the free flow of people — individual mobility. It also contains a comparative analysis of economic unions, both within nation states and between nation states. Thomas J. Courchene's monograph, *Economic Management and the Division of Powers* (Volume 67), and that by John Whalley, *Regional Aspects of Confederation* (Volume 68), round out the series.

Each of these volumes deals in part with aspects of negative integration — the attempts within economic unions to prevent the erection of barriers between original constituent parts. As well, many of the papers look at the positive aspects of the economic union, the attempts to arrive at common policies to promote a particular social or economic interest or concern.

*Mobility of Capital in the Canadian Economic Union* breaks new ground in Canadian studies. The concern for both capital and labour mobility emerged as an issue in the 1970s when a number of highly visible government actions led academics and then governments to express concern as to the effectiveness of Canadian law in ensuring that the benefits to be derived from the mobility of capital and people within the federation are maximized. Because each initiative by government had both regional supporters and national detractors, and as the constitutional negotiations moved mobility onto the "Rights" agenda, the need for some analysis of its underpinnings in Canadian law led to the preparation of this study.

The issue of mobility is one of very real current concern. The debate on the regulation of the Canadian financial market, as well as the question of regional ownership and control of major pools of capital, has generated concern as to the ability of the provinces to lead private actors and investors into economically efficient decisions. The appropriate jurisdictional line between the federal and provincial governments has been the subject of hearings and policy papers by the federal government and the provinces. Industry has joined in calling for greater harmonization between orders of government as well as between the provinces.

The Canadian financial markets are not subject solely to control within Canada by Canadian governments; they also respond to international pressures and trends, which must be taken into account by a small country such as Canada. This volume provides a comprehensive framework as to the ways in which governments can respond, given the tools available to them in the Constitution.

The approach taken in this monograph reflects a need to try to understand the Constitution in theory and practice. The study addresses the range of powers available to respective governments and then looks again at the limits to which governments have gone to utilize levers traditionally thought to be outside their responsibility — to see, in other words, whether the constitutional text can be circumvented by the actions of government. As well, the study looks at developing areas of controversy in the financial field to try to position the debate for the next amendments to the *Bank Act*. At stake is the use of vast pools of capital. It will be an area in which we may soon again see constitutional litigation.

MARK KRASNICK

# ACKNOWLEDGMENTS

The author wishes to thank the following people for their helpful advice; members of the Commission's Research Advisory Group; Yves Lemay, Director of the Legal Department of the Laurentian Group Corporation; François Chevrette, Dean of the Faculty of Law at the University of Montreal; and Ivan Bernier, the Commission's research director for law and constitutional issues. He also wishes to thank Carlotta Lemieux, Dan Liebman and Ann Woollcombe for editorial assistance.

This is a translation of the French-language text which was completed in December 1984 but refers to studies published after that date — *The Regulation of Canadian Financial Institutions: Proposals for Discussion* published in April 1985 by the Department of Finance, and *A Regulatory Framework for Entry into and Ownership of the Ontario Securities Industry* published in February 1985 by the Ontario Securities Commission — regarding the ownership of brokerage firms and the exemption to the rules of registration of securities allowed by the Ontario legislature.

# Introduction

## The Free Movement of Capital: The Reality

The issue of the free movement of capital in Canada[1] has received very little attention in textbooks and in Canadian case law. This indifference is probably due to the predominance of private transactions in the Canadian economy and the relative weakness of government intervention in national economic activity. However, increased government intervention since World War II and the evolution of the Canadian social, political, and economic fabric give rise to increasingly frequent controversies (not all of them significant) which touch directly or indirectly on the issue of the benefits of the free movement of capital within the Canadian economic union. Some recent events that should be considered are:

- the appearance (and increasing number) of large institutional investors, which has altered the financial markets;
- the weakening of the "four pillars" principle, which defines the respective roles of the various financial institutions (underwriting securities for brokerage firms, insurance for insurance companies, commercial credit for banks, and trust activities for trust companies) in favour of a functional interpenetration of traditional areas of activity;
- the debate on the de facto existence of a national securities market and on the degree of uniformity required in regulating it;
- the rapid introduction of data-processing equipment, which requires a re-examination of the roles of Parliament and the legislatures with respect to the various types of transaction at issue;

- the apparent lack of coordination in fiscal policy between the federal government and certain provinces; and
- the implementation of certain measures designed to control direct investment that originates either abroad or within the Canadian union.

## The Movement of Capital Within the Canadian Economic Union

Although the Canadian Constitution is not specific about the degree of economic integration which underlies it, the courts have generally given interpretations that favour the development of an economic union.[2]

The concept of economic union was originally based on the theory of trade.[3] But whereas this theory includes only the free movement of goods, economic union also includes the free movement of labour and capital.[4] Some of the groups that appeared before the Royal Commission on the Economic Union and Development Prospects for Canada echoed this theory in suggesting that favouring the free movement of capital within the Canadian economic union is a priority.[5]

Distortions in the marketplace are generally perceived as being obstacles, barriers. Barriers which interfere with the free movement of capital will limit the supposed advantages of specialized production and trade between provinces.[6] In fact, the economic effects of distortion are not necessarily negative. Most economists feel that distortion is the result of discriminatory policies whereby the parties to a transaction are not all treated in the same way. Such policies may be explicit or implicit, and their effects may be stimulating or restrictive.[7] When the authorities intervene in the marketplace, it is often in order to correct its imperfections, and therefore this does not necessarily create real obstacles to the free movement of capital.[8]

This monograph describes, first of all, the respective areas of jurisdiction of Parliament and the legislatures as related in some way to the movement of capital within the Canadian economy. In Chapter 1 we offer an assessment of the present division of responsibilities between these two levels of government and attempt to define the constitutional limitations of their mutual intervention. In Chapter 2 we examine the regulation of financial institutions and look at the actual sharing of responsibility for the supervision of such institutions between the federal and provincial authorities; in particular, we examine the issue of subjecting all deposit institutions to banking legislation, the rapid diversification of the activities of financial institutions, and the dominant influence of institutional investors on financial markets. In Chapter 3 we look at the influence which certain interest groups derive from the fact that their mutual relationships actually create networks, and we relate these hidden forces to the obligation of the public authorities to ensure that the public interest is respected by means of restrictive regulation and direct intervention in the marketplace. Finally, in Chapter 4, we analyze the suggestions for reform that were put forward at the time of the constitutional negotiations in 1980–81 with a view to entrenching in the Constitution itself the principle of the free movement of capital within the Canadian economic union.

# Chapter 1

# The Free Movement of Capital in Canada:
## *Constitutional Aspects*

### The Silence of the Constitution

The Constitution does not expressly recognize the principle of the free movement of capital within the Canadian economic union.[9] In effect, section 121 of the *Constitution Act, 1867* is aimed primarily at the elimination of customs barriers which are likely to interfere with the movement of goods between provinces. It is only recently that an argument based on a liberal interpretation of Supreme Court decisions has been used in support of this provision in order to remove both federal and provincial non-tariff barriers to the free movement of goods.[10] Even if we agree with this school of thought, it would appear that it applies only to the movement of goods, since the term "article" in s.121 of the act does not include capital as a factor of production.

The recent enactment of the *Canadian Charter of Rights and Freedoms* does not seem to have changed the situation; in fact, the free movement of capital is not one of the principles entrenched in the Constitution by the Charter. It can be argued that the guarantees provided in s.6 of the Charter give every citizen or permanent resident of Canada the right "to move to and take up residence in any province" and "to pursue the gaining of a livelihood in any province," establishing the right (which binds both the legislative assemblies and governments, federal as well as provincial) to bring in and remove capital from any province without impediment,[11] subject to the exceptions in s.6(3) and (4). This interpretation is interesting, but it is incidental to the constitutional debates of 1980–81, in which the liberalization of the movement of capital was considered in the context of expanding s.121 of the *Constitution Act, 1867*, rather than in the context of inserting it in the Charter.

The issue was finally abandoned in the political debate of the day, and to insist too vigorously on expanding the scope of s.6 as a means of promoting the free movement of capital would amount to ignoring the intention of the parties to that debate. In fact, it would probably be wrong to presume that the drafters intended this section as the embryo of a charter of individual economic rights; rather, it reflects a desire to provide a means of combatting obstacles to the free movement of capital in the context of improving the foundations of the Canadian economic union. In addition, expanding the scope of s.6 to cover the movement of capital would probably only affect individuals and not legal entities, and it would only remove obstacles set up by legislatures and governments.[12] A reserved approach on the part of the courts would therefore appear to be preferable, especially since neither Parliament nor the legislature can, with respect to this provision of the Charter, exercise the right to override, which was provided for in s.33. Consequently, the only escape available, aside from those provided for in s. 6(3) and (4), is that in s.1.

In addition to the guarantees provided by s.6 with respect to personal mobility, it has already been suggested that the legal guarantee of the right to security of the person, mentioned in s.7 of the Charter, includes protection of the right to property. Not only individuals but also legal entities would benefit from such protection. However, such an interpretation, as suggested by Mr. Justice Dixon of the New Brunswick Court of Queen's Bench in *The Queen v. Fishermen's Wharf Ltd.*, would seem to ignore the intention of those who drafted the Charter, since they expressly avoided formal insertion of the right to property. However, as Professor Whyte suggests, a reasonable interpretation of the right to security of the person can legitimately include certain economic aspects, such as the right to engage in a given economic activity or the right to possess certain goods.[13] Finally, it can be argued that the right to "liberty" provided for in s.7 of the Charter guarantees each person the freedom to do as he wishes with his capital — provided, of course, that the right is exercised "in accordance with the principles of fundamental justice."

In fact, extending the scope of the right to "liberty" in such a way brings up the issue of the real significance of s.6 of the Charter, which deals specifically with mobility rights. Indeed, it would have been very curious had the federal and provincial authorities finally decided upon a restrictive formulation of the right to circulate, as provided for in s.6, while in the same breath guaranteeing concurrently and implicitly, in s.7 of the Charter, the very same principle of the free movement of individuals and capital throughout Canada (including intraprovincially). A possible means of reconciling these two provisions in such a case would be to conclude that s.6 establishes the minimum parameters of mobility rights (legislative assemblies would not be able to use s.33 to circumvent this provision), and that s.7 opens the door to a more generous interpretation of this right by the courts, and thus the legislatures are free to express their disagreement if need be. In addition, the nature of the guarantee provided for in s.7 appears to be simply procedural, and this may explain the more extensive scope of mobility rights which the latter section is supposed to provide. However, confirmation by the courts of the substantive nature of the guarantees mentioned in s.7 would seriously weaken the value of such an argument.

On the other hand, s.15 of the Charter establishes the principle of equality before the law "without discrimination and, in particular, without discrimination based on race, national or ethnic origin, colour, religion, sex, age or mental or physical disability." The scope of this guarantee has not yet been defined, but it can reasonably be expected that Parliament and the provincial legislatures would not use such grounds of discrimination as criteria applicable to provisions dealing with the movement of capital. In any case, the guarantees provided for in ss.7 and 15 are subject to the general exception in s.1 of the Charter and can be overridden, either by Parliament or by a provincial legislature, by a simple declaration of withdrawal in application of s.33.

Finally, it should be noted that the *Canadian Bill of Rights* and certain provincial charters of rights expressly include the right to property. Nevertheless, the relevant provisions of these documents are probably just procedural guarantees which do not in themselves affect the sovereign right of the legislatures to exercise their powers fully.[14]

In short, without an effective framework that imposes the principle of the free movement of capital within the economic union, legislative assemblies and the federal and provincial governments can regulate its movement at their pleasure within the inherent limits of their respective powers. Consequently, we consider that it is essential to analyze the division of constitutional jurisdiction between Ottawa and the provinces in order to be able to assess their present or future intervention in the capital markets.

## Federal Powers

### *The Canadian Monetary Union*

The central government has been given paramount economic powers which ensure that it has the necessary authority to control the Canadian monetary union unilaterally; in other words, it has the power to enact, within the context of a common market, a single currency and a single rate of exchange.[15] Indeed, the *Constitution Act, 1867* gives Parliament exclusive legislative jurisdiction with respect to currency and exchange, legal tender, banks, savings banks, bills of exchange and promissory notes, interest and the issue of paper money, and the regulation of trade and commerce.[16] Thus, by the terms of s.91(14) and (15) of the *Constitu-*

*tion Act, 1867*, the provinces cannot in any way regulate the movement of capital through the control of exchange rates. Parliament thus seems to possess all the constitutional tools necessary to maintain the integrity of the Canadian monetary union.[17]

In addition, the Supreme Court of Canada did not hesitate, in the case of the *Alberta Statutes Reference*, to invoke federal jurisdiction in order to prevent the erosion or disintegration of the Canadian monetary union. During the 1930s, the legislative assembly of Alberta adopted a program whose main effect was to create a new form of credit and currency in Alberta, and whose success depended on the population's confidence that the province would guarantee payments. This parallel system, which was clearly designed to circumvent the national banking system, thus infringed upon it.[18] Almost half a century after the *Alberta Statutes Reference*, the Supreme Court reaffirmed the validity of that position in its decision in *Canadian Pioneer Management Ltd.*[19] Earlier, in the decision in the *Re Anti-Inflation Act*, four of the nine Supreme Court justices had emphasized the global and extensive power of Parliament with respect to currency: since inflation was a monetary phenomenon, Parliament therefore had the power to act to control it.[20]

Similarly, during the 1930s, certain provincial bills, which were aimed at reducing the burden of borrowers who were required to repay capital and to pay interest on their debts, were declared invalid with respect to interest, since these bills infringed upon Parliament's jurisdiction over interest.[21] On the other hand, this power does not allow Parliament to regulate the terms and conditions of loans.

The Canadian Constitution mentions certain types of money instrument, such as paper money, bills of exchange, promissory notes, and legal tender, but it does not seem that federal jurisdiction is limited to the above; federal jurisdiction over "banking" and the "incorporation of banks" reinforces Parliament's position should it want to regulate all instruments. Thus, in the not too distant future, electronic tranfers of funds could become the most common method of payment and could change the basic nature of a negotiable instrument. We can already foresee certain parallels, such as the functional parallel between electronic transfers of funds and bills of exchange or legal tender.[22] On the other hand, the Canadian Bar Association has already clearly expressed the opinion that the maintenance of the monetary union necessitates federal control over the transfer of electronic funds.[23]

## *Banking*

Since legislative jurisdiction over banking and the incorporation of banks was deemed to be inseparable from the responsibilities of administering the monetary union, the *Constitution Act, 1867* attributed such jurisdiction to the federal authorities. Indeed, we must not forget that until the Bank of Canada was established by the 1934 *Bank of Canada Act*, private banks issued currency and were closely linked to the development, formulation, and application of the government's monetary policy.

Although s.91(15) of the *Constitution Act, 1867* is precise and brief, it is not surprising that one of the most lively controversies surrounding economic constitutional law concerned the definition of the respective areas of jurisdiction of Parliament and the provincial legislatures regarding the financial activities of banks, near-banks,[24] and other financial intermediaries in general. Thus, the problem is not so much the precision of the wording of the Constitution but the absence of a definition of the "business of banking."[25] In 1894 the Privy Council, in the decision in *Tennant v. Union Bank of Canada*, affirmed that the business of banking was "wide enough to embrace every transaction coming within the legitimate business of a banker."[26] Half a century later, the same court, in the decision in *A.-G. Alberta v. A.-G. Canada*, held that Parliament had exclusive jurisdiction over activities that were an integral part of "banking" and that this was not limited only to the activities and operations of banks in 1867.[27]

Various definitions, both jurisprudential and doctrinal, have been suggested for the concept of the "business of banking" from different points of view, such as the relationship between the institution and its clients, the functional test on a legal or economic level, the formal test, and the institutional test.

Thus Mr. Justice Beetz of the Supreme Court of Canada, in the decision in *Canadian Pioneer Management Ltd.*, thought it appropriate to point out that certain operations carried out by banks fulfil the role of a fiduciary (or a mandatory) rather than a bank; this is the case when they issue travellers cheques or when they are intermediaries for the sale of registered home-ownership savings plans or registered retirement savings plans.[28] It has been said that distinguishing the nature of the relationship between a bank and its client, and that of a trust company and its client has virtually no constitutional significance.[29] On the other hand, the Supreme Court pointed out in the above-mentioned decision that although it is not conclusive, it is a factor which allows them to be distinguished in the process of determining constitutional jurisdiction.[30] In the recently published *Working Document on the Revision of the Trust Companies Act and the Loan Companies Act*, the federal Department of Insurance suggested that the concept of a guaranteed trust for deposits accepted by federal trust companies should be abandoned in favour of a debtor-creditor relationship, as in the case of mortgage loan companies and banks.[31] The Ontario government's white paper on the revision of its loan and trust corporation legislation described this proposal as "ill advised," since it tended to deny the specific nature of a trust company's relationship with its clients.[32]

In the *Alberta Statutes Reference*, Mr. Justice Duff and Mr. Justice Kerwin of the Supreme Court, using a functionalist approach, also tried to define the specific nature of the business of banking in terms of economics.[33] Lord Porter, in the case of *A.-G. Canada v. A.-G. Quebec*, expanded upon those views as follows:

> The receipt of deposits and the repayment of the sums deposited to the depositors or their successors as defined above is an essential part of the business of banking.[34]

Applied literally, in the context of modern economics, this definition in itself could mean that all institutions operating as deposit and credit institutions, such as provincial trust companies and caisses populaires, would be considered as banks. The Supreme Court refused to do this in the *Canadian Pioneer Management Ltd.* case. Mr. Justice Beetz, citing Mr. Justice Richards of the Manitoba Court of Appeal in *Re Bergethaler Waisemant*, concluded that the simple fact that a bank performs various kinds of financial operation does not give it an exclusive right over each of them (such as chequing account services). In short, noting that the functional test would place caisses populaires and provincial trust companies under federal jurisdiction, the Supreme Court abandoned it in favour of the formal test and the institutional test.[35]

In the context of banking, these criteria led the courts to conclude that a bank is an institution which is authorized to represent itself as a bank and which has acquired the reputation of being a bank. Thus, the *Bank Act* identifies by name those institutions authorized to use the name "bank" and stipulates the penalties imposed for the name's unauthorized use.[36] If Parliament does not deem it opportune to include an institution in the list of banks, it may be concluded that the institution is not a bank for the purposes of s.91(15). The Supreme Court is unanimous on this point.[37] Conversely, although it is not certain, it may be said that the fact that an institution is called a bank by the federal authorities establishes in a conclusive fashion that it is a bank and that it therefore comes exclusively within Parliament's legislative jurisdiction. On the other hand, the fact that banks are authorized to carry out certain types of operation does not necessarily make them "banking businesses." This would make those financial institutions within provincial jurisdiction which also perform this type of operation subject to federal regulation.[38] This distinction is crucial in the context of the actual extension of banking activities to certain areas occupied by other financial intermediaries, such as stockbrokers.

In short, s.91(15) of the *Constitution Act, 1867* gives Parliament exclusive legislative jurisdiction over banks. However, the definition of the "business of banking" remains evolutionary and vague. Since the Supreme Court of Canada's decision in the *Canadian Pioneer Management Ltd.* case, the formal and institutional tests are of primary importance in identifying a bank, though the functional test has not been completely abandoned, and an analysis of the relationship between the institution and the client is still relevant. Certain financial institutions that come under provincial jurisdiction (such as caisses populaires and trust companies) could therefore be considered by Parliament to be banks. This possibility would provide the federal government with a powerful means of intervening should a situation arise in which, when regulating near-banks, a province created obstacles that were deemed unacceptable for the free movement of capital. In addition, it would seem that s.91(15) of the *Constitution Act, 1867* gives Parliament complete and exclusive jurisdiction to regulate the processing of the enormous amount of data gathered by banks.[39]

Nevertheless, banks are subject to provincial laws, with the following exceptions: laws whose basic purpose is to regulate the field of banking; laws which, although valid, derogate from the banks' basic powers; and laws which are incompatible with federal banking legislation.[40]

## The Free Movement of Capital and Federal Economic Powers

Aside from the powers related to the administration of the monetary union and the regulation of the field of banking, the Canadian Constitution gives Parliament several other economic powers which it can invoke in order to regulate the movement of capital, either directly or indirectly within the context of various economic policies.

### THE REGULATION OF TRADE AND COMMERCE

Section 91(2) of the *Constitution Act, 1867* gives Parliament legislative jurisdiction over the regulation of trade and commerce. This provision has had an eventful jurisprudential and doctrinal history.[41] In the famous case of *Citizens' Insurance Company of Canada v. Parsons*, the Privy Council held that there were two aspects to federal jurisdiction in this case: the power to regulate international and interprovincial commerce; and "general trade power" in the national interest.[42] This general power does not, however, justify the regulation of a particular commercial activity or industry. Until the 1950s, the applicability of the commerce clause had not really been expanded,[43] although it should be pointed out that during this period it was cited by three of the six Supreme Court judges in the *Alberta Statutes Reference* case to confirm the predominant responsibility of the federal government in the administration of the Canadian monetary union.[44]

It is not clear that the first aspect of the *Parsons* case can be relied on by Parliament to regulate the movement of capital, since it seems to apply only to the movement of goods.[45] On the other hand, the second aspect would certainly offer effective protection against provincial measures which are deemed unacceptable for the free movement of capital by means of the applicability test established by case law.[46] The decision in the *Alberta Statutes Reference* is an eloquent precedent in this regard.[47] Professors Anisman and Hogg have become the champions of the constitutional validity of future federal securities legislation based on Parliament's general power of economic regulation.[48] Mr. Justice Dickson of the Supreme Court, in the case of *Multiple Access Ltd. v. McCutcheon*, recently demonstrated his open-mindedness on the prospect of a federal administrative regime for the securities market, and Mr. Justice Estey (dissenting) expanded on his colleague's remarks, saying that it would be inappropriate to dismiss the possibility of parliamentary intervention in the regulation of the securities market.[49] However, the provinces have regulated this sector for more than seventy years and they have developed a cooperative interprovincial network.[50] It should be pointed out that even if a federal law does overcome all obstacles, as the Supreme Court has implied, it is doubtful that it could be applied to purely intraprovincial operations.[51]

The same ambiguity exists with respect to extending the federal government's general power over commerce to the regulation of mutual funds[52] or to control over foreign investment. In the latter case, even if it can be claimed that the *Foreign Investment Review Act* respects all the criteria of the *Vapor Canada Ltd.* case,[53] it remains to be proven, if future case law upholds Mr. Justice Dickson's views in the case of *Canadian National Transportation Ltd.*, that legislatures may not control foreign investment or that the Constitution does not empower the provinces to enact such a law, jointly or separately.

Finally, the relevance of s.91(2) of the *Constitution Act, 1867* as a mechanism for the maintenance or encouragement of the free movement of capital seems to flow logically from the Supreme Court decision in the case of *Canadian Industrial Gas and Oil Ltd. v. Government of Saskatchewan*. In effect, this decision provides a concrete illustration of a case in which provincial legislative measures can possibly infringe upon the harmonious operation of the economic union. In relying on the commerce clause to reject the fiscal measures by which the Province of Saskatchewan tried to keep almost all of the excess profits resulting from the phenomenal increase in the price of oil, the court seems to have shown considerable concern for what the effect would be on the balance of Canadian federalism if a province acquired an enormous accumulation of capital; this, in spite of the fact that the measures adopted by Saskatchewan were a logical consequence of the right to property and the administration of natural resources which the Constitution grants to the provinces. If, in this particular case, the accumulation of capital was enough to justify recourse to the commerce clause, then it is conceivable that the highest court would also readily rely on the clause to quash provincial regulations which interfere with the interprovincial or international movement of capital and which prevent the economic union from functioning properly.[54]

## Peace, Order and Good Government

The preamble to s.91 of the *Constitution Act, 1867* gave Parliament the power to legislate for "the Peace, Order and Good Government of Canada."[55] This power is primarily designed to deal with exceptional situations which would not be covered by an explicit list, for example, the incorporation of federal commercial companies or the establishment of an official languages scheme in federal institutions.[56] In addition, it is accepted that emergency situations in time of peace or war justify Parliament using this power to legislate on matters which would otherwise come under the exclusive jurisdiction of the provincial legislatures. The most striking example of this in recent years has undoubtedly been the Supreme Court of Canada's decision with regard to the *Anti-Inflation Act*. This decision upheld the constitutionality of federal wage and price controls. Nevertheless, the nine Supreme Court judges unanimously confirmed the view that any provision enacted pursuant to an emergency power could only be valid for a limited period of time.[57]

On the other hand, recent Supreme Court decisions have exacerbated the persistent theoretical ambiguity with respect to the interpretation of the "national concern"[58] aspect, and consequently this concept is now too vague to enable us to assess the potential effect on the division of powers between Parliament and the provincial legislatures.

In spite of these uncertainties, Parliament's power to legislate for the peace, order and good government of Canada constitutes a specific fall-back position for the federal government should it choose to intervene to protect the free movement of capital within the Canadian economic union. In fact, Parliament could probably invoke an "emergency" situation in order to impose draconian measures which would infringe upon even the explicit powers of the provinces; all that is required is that it be proven that a state of emergency exists and that the measures taken be of limited duration. A good example of this is the anti-inflation measures which were held to be constitutional: the *Anti-Inflation Act* even authorized the Governor in Council to prescribe restraining guidelines for dividends.[59] In an emergency situation, Parliament could, it seems, enact measures affecting any aspect of the use of capital, both its movement within and outside the country and the sharing of local or foreign credit markets among potential borrowers.

As far as the "national concern" aspect of the right to legislate for peace, order, and good government is concerned, it would seem to be too vague to allow the federal government to intervene in the regulation of those financial sectors which at present come under provincial jurisdiction. Thus, it is unlikely that the regulation of the securities market, a traditionally provincial domain, could in this way come under federal jurisdiction,[60] since the provinces have already implemented a detailed system of interprovincial cooperation in this area. In fact, the desire to standardize legislation in a particular area does not in itself justify the transfer of legislative responsibility to Parliament, as Chief Justice Laskin quite rightly pointed out in *Re Anti-Inflation Act*.[61] This reasoning is particularly relevant in areas where interprovincial cooperation has been a fact of life for decades. Similarly, the insurance industry seems to be protected from "national" intervention. At the beginning of the century, while emphasizing the very considerable importance of this sector, the Supreme Court of Canada, in *Re Insurance Act, 1910*, confirmed that it came under provincial jurisdiction.[62] Since then, provincial jurisdiction in this area has never really been disputed, and the Supreme Court has been quick to reject any claim to the contrary.[63]

### The Federal Power to Incorporate Companies

The enumerated powers which the Constitution specifically confers on Parliament do not include the power to incorporate commercial companies, with the exception of banks. The courts corrected this oversight in giving Parliament this prerogative on the basis of its power to legislate for the peace, order, and good government of Canada, and on the basis of ss.91(29) and 92(10), which deal with interprovincial corporations in the fields of transportation or communications. It is, however, generally felt that the power to incorporate companies cannot be linked to the federal power over trade and commerce.[64] The incorporation of a company is clearly distinguishable from the regulation of its activities;[65] it consists of creating a new legal entity subject to company law, with the powers and obligations that this entails, especially with respect to internal regulation (maintenance of the company, protection of creditors and shareholders, and the eligibility and supervision of directors) and financing. Parliament's power to incorporate companies includes the power to prescribe conditions for the transfer of shares of the share capital of federally incorporated companies. However, the exact scope of the power to incorporate companies remains vague, since it changes with the socioeconomic situation.[66]

The power to regulate the activities of federally incorporated companies is shared pursuant to the Constitution. Thus, the Privy Council and the Supreme Court of Canada have upheld the enforceability, against federally incorporated companies, of provincial laws which give a Crown corporation in the province in question a monopoly over automobile insurance,[67] or which regulate the acquisition of real property,[68] and even those which prevent a company from issuing securities publicly without going through a broker who holds the appropriate provincial licence.[69] In addition, in the case of *Société Asbestos Limitée v. Société nationale de l'amiante*, the Quebec Court of Appeal confirmed the validity of the expropriation of the assets of a federally incorporated company by a provincial authority under a specific provincial statute.[70] The Supreme Court recently reaffirmed this principle in the case of *Re Upper Churchill Water Rights Reservation Act*.[71] Briefly, the court held as follows:

> Provincial legislation may license and regulate the activities of federal companies within the field of provincial competence and may impose sanctions for the enforcement of its regulations, but such sanctions may not be such as to strike at the essential capacities and status of a federal company. In exercising its legislative powers, however, the provincial legislature may not venture into the field of company law in respect of the federal company. It may not legislate so as to affect the corporate structure of the federal entity or so as to render the federal company incapable of creating its corporate being and exercising its essential corporate powers as a company.[72]

This immunity is particularly obvious when the capacity of such companies to finance themselves is threatened.

In certain questionable cases, the federal government can make use of company law to extend its powers of control and surveillance over a given sector. Thus, the organization of investment companies which have been incorporated pursuant to federal legislation is governed by the *Investment Companies Act*. Certain provisions of this act have the effect of limiting the participation of non-residents in the share-capital of these companies.[73] A similar phenomenon exists with respect to federal life insurance companies and federal trust companies. In addition, the general regime of company law, as established by the *Canada Business Corporations Act*, provides that a majority of directors of companies incorporated pursuant to this act must be resident Canadians.[74] Another clear example of the importance of controlling the terms and conditions of company law is the fact that Parliament amended this act in 1982 in order to enable federally incorporated companies to hold shares in themselves, to convert them into shares subject to restrictions, and to resell them in order to be in conformity with the conditions of Canadian participation, which entails the right to certain advantages (such as those provided by the National Energy Program of 1980).[75]

On the other hand, Parliament can require that a party that wants to operate in a field of activity which comes under federal jurisdiction, by virtue of s.91 of the Canadian Constitution, must be incorporated pursuant to its legislation. In this way, Parliament has control over the powers and internal operations of such companies, and in general of anything that comes under the heading of company law. In fields of banking, transportation, and communications that are within its competence, Parliament has not hesitated to make use of its prerogatives in order to add to several legislative provisions which affect these various sectors — either provisions which reserve to federal companies the right to operate in these sectors or various controls which regulate foreign investment or the transfer of corporate control.[76] While they may seem clear, the legality and legitimacy of the controls imposed on banks, and on interprovincial or international transportation or communications companies, become complex when they are applied, directly or indirectly, to investment companies or to conglomerates which have only one relatively unimportant activity in this category. The recent polemic raised by Bill S-31 (*Act to limit shareholding in certain corporations*) illustrates the complexity of the phenomenon. While it was officially justified by the need to protect interprovincial transportation companies from being controlled by one or more of the provinces acting as shareholders, the prohibition imposed on the provinces from directly or indirectly controlling more than 10 percent of any class of share of such corporations[77] has blocked them, de facto, not only from this type of investment but also from the possibility of participating in the share-capital of such holding companies and, indirectly, from that of numerous and important companies (affiliated or linked to these companies) which do not come under the exclusive legislative jurisdiction of Parliament.[78]

The spillover effects of the power to incorporate companies, associated with an enumerated power — ss.91(15), 91(29) and 92(10) of the *Constitution Act, 1867* — literally gives Parliament the discretion to ensure corporate control of a large portion of economic activity. The tendency of public service companies to diversify their corporate activities is a recent phenomenon[79] and does not appear to have been of particular concern to the courts (aside from many decisions in the field of labour relations) in the context of evaluating the "exclusive" right of Parliament to regulate the companies concerned.

The key Privy Council or Supreme Court decisions which uphold the integrity of the interprovincial transportation networks and the exclusiveness[80] of Parliament's jurisdiction to regulate them were rendered at a time when the companies involved really only operated in areas and activities within the jurisdiction of Parliament. Since this situation has changed rapidly during the last few years, the scope of these decisions should be re-examined in light of the new circumstances. In addition, if it is assumed that control measures similar to those contained in Bill S-31 are constitutional, then it is possible that the provincial legislatures would counter with similar measures with respect to companies authorized to do business in areas of activity within their jurisdiction. Thus, it is conceivable that one or more of the provinces would try to restrict to provincially incorporated companies the privilege of holding mining, forestry, or oil leases with respect to the development of their public domain, and that they would prohibit direct or indirect participation by federal authorities in the share-capital of such companies. In light of the very limited immunity of federal companies from provincial legislation, such action would probably be considered valid, especially if the provinces only acted as market participants in the agreement, as opposed to intervening by means of regulation. However, if such a phenomenon produced intolerable consequences, it is possible that the courts would rely on the (negative) commerce clause in order to put a stop to such practices, or even that Parliament would legislate positively in this regard by virtue of the same clause.

As far as mutual funds are concerned, the obligation to be incorporated pursuant to federal law will take on particular importance, since the very existence of such companies depends on their ability to increase their shareholders' assets.[81] Similarly, it is doubtful that a provincial legislature could subject the transfer of the shares of a federally incorporated company to its general regulations pertaining to the activities of trust and loan companies, as the Government of Ontario suggested in its white paper on such companies. Indeed, the Government of Ontario suggested that all loan and trust companies "registered to do business in Ontario" should be subject to the provisions of the *Loan and Trust Corporations Act* with respect to share transfers.[82]

## International Treaties

With the exception of s.132 of the *Constitution Act, 1867*, which provides that the "Parliament and Government of Canada shall have all Powers necessary or proper for performing the Obligations of Canada or of any Province thereof, as Part of the British Empire, towards Foreign Countries, arising under Treaties between the Empire and such Foreign Countries,"[83] the Constitution is silent with regard to granting to one or other level of government specific jurisdiction over external affairs. Despite this, since 1926 the federal government has, for all practical purposes, become the master of Canada's foreign policy, and it has the capability of signing binding international agreements on its own account.[84]

The enforcement of international agreements in domestic law parallels the sharing of legislative jurisdiction between Parliament and the provincial legislatures. If the object of the agreement falls within provincial jurisdiction, then it is up to each of the provinces to enact and promulgate the relevant legislation; on the other hand, if Parliament has jurisdiction, then it may legislate to enforce the agreement.[85] However, the majority decision handed down by Mr. Justice Laskin, in the case of *MacDonald v. Vapor Canada Ltd.*, contains indications that the Supreme Court would be inclined to alter the direction of the Privy Council decision in the *Labour Conventions* case in order to recognize, on the grounds of Parliament's power to legislate for the peace, order, and good government of Canada, that it can give effect, in domestic law, to the provisions of international treaties to which Canada is a party.[86] Recently, Mr. Justice Dickson of the Supreme Court considered the suggestion of redefining Parliament's power in this regard, without, however, clearly holding that the Supreme Court was adopting the suggestions of Chief Justice Laskin in the *Vapor Canada Ltd.* case.[87]

In the absence of an international treaty binding it, any sovereign state has, in principle, absolute discretion with respect to opening its markets to foreign investors. However, customary international law (which, of course, a government is not necessarily required to recognize) provides foreign investors with two guarantees by ensuring them protection of their "vested rights" and the absence of discrimination vis-à-vis their investments. Thus, the expropriation of foreign assets should be compensated in short order by sufficient and concrete payment. These principles of international law have been echoed in numerous Canadian laws dealing with foreign investments.[88]

At the regional level, western economic powers have undertaken to free the movement of capital in the context of the Organisation for Economic Co-operation and Development (OECD) by adopting a Code of Liberalization of Capital Movements.[89] This code, which applies to an impressive number of financial operations, is based on the principle of non-discrimination among the various foreign investments, but without guaranteeing equal treatment with national investments.[90] It is remarkable that in the case of a federal nation (for example, the United States), the council of the OECD took into account the particular federal structure of each of the U.S. states. Thus, the code does not supersede the decisions of any individual U.S. state that acts within the limits of its jurisdiction, having agreed, at the request of any member country of OECD which has itself ratified the code, that the United States government must direct the attention of the state concerned to the provisions of the code, must inform it of the alleged harm, and must communicate its own recommendation.[91] At the present time, Canada is not committed to this code and is therefore not bound by it.

In addition to the code, in 1976 the OECD adopted two conventions dealing with the regulation of inducements and restrictions on international investment and on the behaviour of multinationals. However, these documents do not affect the right of member nations to control the entry of foreign investment or to control conditions for setting up foreign companies.[92]

The United States also alleged that another agreement of regional scope, the General Agreement on Tariffs and Trade (GATT), could be used against measures that subject foreign investment to the inclusion of some degree of local content in production or in export objectives. The recent report of a GATT arbitration board on the practices of the Canadian Foreign Investment Review Agency (FIRA) concluded that it was incompatible with the GATT agreements to require foreign investors to commit themselves to purchasing Canadian products or to using Canadian suppliers, but that export commitments were not subject to such agreements.[93] In short, the GATT governs commercial trade but not the national measures of member nations with respect to foreign investment. In addition, it offers no direct recourse to individuals who feel that they have been wronged by one of the member nations.

## Transborder Data Flows

The international movement of data, a contemporary phenomenon, is increasingly important because of the development of ultra-quick communications networks and because of the tendency of corporations to rationalize their activities by creating functional units of operation which do not necessarily coincide with the borders of sovereign states.[94] This situation increases a sovereign state's vulnerability to having strategic data transferred out of its reach. As far as capital is concerned, these new systems, based on computers and on methods of communication, favour the integration and concentration of large financial groups and greater liquidity of capital. The world community is concerned about the consequences of this development and is seeking solutions which involve adopting international measures.[95] In September 1980, the council of the OECD adopted guidelines for the protection of private life and personal transborder data flows;[96] the council has since directed its attention toward the criminal and civil responsibility aspects related to such flows.

Various other international organizations and nations are also studying the numerous factors relating to the international movement of data, which indicates that in the near future a system of international law will be established, and that it could, in its path, reinforce the respective positions of the federal and provincial authorities — for example, international cooperation in the fight against computer crime, the possibility of adopting the principle of the free movement of data between countries, the protection of personal or strategic data, and the protection of intellectual property.

## Taxation

Section 91(3) of the *Constitution Act, 1867* gives Parliament the power to raise money "by any Mode or System of Taxation."[97] This power is not restricted either territorially or functionally, except by the usual principles of constitutional interpretation. Thus, the doctrine of disguised legislation has been relied upon to overrule a federal tax which was deemed to constitute an attempt to regulate the insurance market.[98] Nevertheless, the courts are very hesitant to denounce a federal tax provision as such. The federal power to tax is limited by provincial immunity from taxation, as provided in s.125 of the *Constitution Act, 1867*, but this immunity can be avoided if the fiscal measures are intended not only as a means of collecting revenue but also as a means of regulating the economy.[99]

The federal government's unlimited and flexible power to impose taxes allows it not only to collect the revenue that it requires but also to channel financial resources toward the economic objectives that it has set. For example, in 1983 the minister of finance, Marc Lalonde, applied fiscal measures to research and development; and in 1984, as a measure of pension reform, he proposed a plan of action that included a tax assistance scheme to improve retirement savings.[100]

It should be pointed out that the federal government has, in the past, made use of its powers of taxation in such a way as to shape the fiscal pie in terms of provincial boundaries. Thus, in the context of the National Energy Program of 1980, it unilaterally created a tax scheme, in which the expenditures incurred for developing "Canadian" land were given more favourable treatment than those for developing provincial land. The economist Thomas J. Courchene observed:

> The provincial response will surely be that if Ottawa, for its own tax purposes, can discriminate on the basis of the location of the economic activity, so can the provinces.[101]

Thus, the power of taxation is at the very heart of federal industrial policy, and it explains the resistance and frustration of certain provinces. The Government of Alberta, in its 1984 white paper on industrial and scientific policy, did not hide the impatience it felt at the seeming insensitivity of federal taxation policies with respect to the economic development of the province. By way of reprisal, it threatened to set up its own personal income tax scheme, as it had done in 1978 in the case of corporate income tax.[102]

## Naturalization and Aliens

One might think that Parliament is empowered to determine the terms and conditions of access of foreign capital to Canadian financial markets because of its legislative jurisdiction over naturalization and aliens.[103] However, since the courts have not yet been called upon to determine the constitutionality of the *Foreign Investment Review Act*, it is not possible to assess the validity of this argument. In fact, it seems that the federal government does not intend to base this legislation primarily on its jurisdiction over aliens but on its general power of economic regulation or on its power to legislate for the peace, order, and good government of Canada. In any case, the Progressive Conservative government elected in 1984 has clearly indicated its intention to reorient the objectives of the Foreign Investment Review Agency, which will henceforth be known as Investment Canada.[104]

## Criminal Law

Section 91(27) of the *Constitution Act, 1867* gives Parliament legislative jurisdiction over criminal law, including criminal procedure, while the provinces have responsibility for the administration of justice within their own territory. The legitimacy of the federal regulation of commercial activities that are contrary to the public interest (such as false or misleading advertising and the fraudulent use of a brand name) is well established in constitutional law. Consequently, the Supreme Court has upheld the Criminal Code provisions which deal with the manufacture, distribution, and publication of false prospectuses of stock issues.[105] However, Parliament could not support legislation whose purpose is economic regulation on its exclusive jurisdiction over criminal law[106] even though that jurisdiction has already been invoked, and could in future be invoked, for the adoption of a federal securities act. Thus, Professors Anisman and Hogg have been equivocal about the extent of the constitutional protection provided by the criminal law for potential federal securities legislation.[107] As regards investment funds, the criminal law seems to support federal legislation which deals with prohibiting fraudulent commercial practices. Finally, with respect to the electronic transfer of funds, the criminal law serves as a basis for the regulation of those aspects of fraud or theft that are related to the collection, storage, or dissemination of information.[108]

### Interprovincial and International Enterprises

Interprovincial or international works and undertakings in the field of transportation and communications come under the constitutional jurisdiction of Parliament by virtue of ss.91(29) and 92(10) of the *Constitution Act, 1867* or by virtue of the general power to legislate for the peace, order, and good government of Canada.[109]

In theory, the declaratory power found in s.92(10)(c) of the *Constitution Act, 1867* allows Parliament to designate an undertaking, which is otherwise of a purely local nature, as being of national interest.[110] Although this power has not been invoked for several decades, it nevertheless exists.

Parliament's firmly established jurisdiction in the field of communications and transportation is reinforced by the fact that the courts tend to refuse to break up the networks. The increased penetration of computers and telecommunications into the financial sector has had a profound effect on relations between the client, the financial institution, and the government, and calls for new intervention on the part of the public authorities.[111] The demarcation between Parliament's constitutional authority and that of the provincial legislatures may be altered as a consequence of the development of interprovincial or international data transfer networks. Thus, the large-scale introduction of automated teller machines (and, in general, the electronic transfer of funds) involves the development of structural elements which favour the expansion of Parliament's jurisdiction.[112]

For those financial institutions which come under provincial jurisdiction, it is likely that the legislatures will maintain regulatory control over the collection, content, and dissemination of information by internal electronic means. However, the development of an electronic interbank network for payments, or the shared use of automated teller machines or direct transfer networks, will further weaken provincial jurisdictional claims (especially where a province has not previously occupied a particular regulatory field).[113]

As far as securities are concerned, s.92(10) of the *Constitution Act, 1867* is crucial for any federal claim to the right to regulate a potential electronic stock exchange network. In 1978, Professors Anisman and Hogg claimed, in a very detailed study, that the operation of stock exchanges in Canada was covered by s.92(10) because the quotation systems of the three largest stock exchanges (Toronto, Montreal and Vancouver) were interconnected, while transactions carried out on the Toronto and Montreal stock exchanges were electronically cleared by the Canadian Depository for Securities, Ltd., and those of the Alberta and Vancouver stock exchanges were cleared by the Vancouver Stock Exchange Service Corporation.[114]

Since then, the computerization of Canadian stock exchanges has advanced considerably. Thus, the Montreal Stock Exchange's MORRE system enables brokers to transmit clients' orders to any Canadian stock exchange in under 30 seconds, at the best cost. In addition, the network of the Montreal Stock Exchange is linked to that of the Boston Stock Exchange, and the Toronto Stock Exchange has announced its intention to link up with the American Exchange, which heralds the integration of the Canadian and American stock exchange networks. The Montreal and Vancouver stock exchanges also deal in options through a centralized computer centre in collaboration with the Sydney (Australia) Stock Exchange and with the European options exchange. The president of the Montreal Stock Exchange has advocated the development of a national market in Canada in which the various Canadian stock exchanges would remove barriers to the movement of data between their respective floors and in which stockbrokers operating in the different exchanges would be in direct competition.[115]

The exclusive legislative jurisdiction provided in s.92(10) also confirms the validity of restrictions on the control of commercial companies in the field of transportation and communications on an interprovincial or international level.[116]

## *Various Powers*

### SPENDING POWER

The federal government can use its spending power[117] to avoid restrictions to its legislative jurisdiction, since it is not required to limit its expenditures to financing activities within its jurisdiction. It is unlikely, however, that an act of Parliament relating to the appropriation of funds would amount to the actual regulation of an area which the Constitution attributes to provincial authorities. Indeed, measures that are designed to control spending are different from measures that are designed to regulate a sector of activity.[118] In addition, s.36 of the *Canadian Charter of Rights and Freedoms*, which deals with the respective obligations of Parliament and the provincial legislatures with regard to equal opportunities and public services, has already caused controversy because of its alleged impact on Parliament's use of its spending power.[119]

This power, like the power of taxation, gives the federal government significant room to manoeuvre in implementing its economic policy, and it makes it possible to create an impressive range of subsidy programs or financial guarantees in favour of the private sector; the federal government has even been able to establish, for its own advantage, discretionary grant schemes (for example, the oil and gas incentive program which was set up in the context of the National Energy Program of 1980 and which includes various benefits, depending on whether the territory is "Canadian" or provincial).[120]

In this context, it is possible that the federal government could use its financial clout to give strong encouragement to the provinces to respect the principle of the free movement of capital by inserting appropriate conditions in fiscal agreements or in agreements to finance established programs.

## BORROWING POWER

Parliament's exclusive legislative authority includes "the Public Debt and Property" and "the borrowing of Money on the Public Credit."[121]

## BANKRUPTCY AND INSOLVENCY

Parliament's legislative jurisdiction over bankruptcy and insolvency can be used to support the expansion of federal influence over capital markets. Thus, in *A.-G. Ontario v. Policy Holders of Wentworth Insurance Co.*,[122] the Supreme Court held that federal legislation with respect to the liquidation of insurance companies predominated over Ontario legislation because of s.91(21) of the *Constitution Act, 1867*. However, it is still not clear that this power could justify the federal regulation of solvent companies in order to prevent insolvencies.[123] However, in promulgating the *Investment Companies Act*, whose purpose was to ensure the solvency of some financial institutions, Parliament did limit the application to federally incorporated financial corporations.[124]

## PENSIONS

The addition of s.94A to the Constitution clarified Parliament's right to regulate old-age pensions and supplementary benefits. The exact scope of this amendment is uncertain, since it is not clear that the new provisions authorize Parliament to regulate all the institutions that operate in this particular field. In fact, s.94A formally specifies that no federal law "shall affect the operation of any law present or future of a provincial legislature in relation to any such matter."[125] In addition to s.94A of the Constitution, Parliament is in a position, by virtue of s.91(8), to regulate "the fixing of and providing for the Salaries and Allowances of Civil and other Officers of the Government of Canada," as well as those of employees of undertakings under the control of the federal government by virtue of s.92(10) or of the "peace, order and good government" clause. The federal government has gained indisputable authority over private pension plans through the Department of National Revenue, which is responsible for the administration of the *Income Tax Act*, which governs the registration of plans, as well as tax deductions, up to a fixed maximum, for payments made to approved plans.

Public retirement pension plans are divided into three main components: old-age security (non-contributory) (OAS), the Guaranteed Income Supplement (non-contributory) (GIS), and the tandem Canada Pension Plan (CPP)/Quebec Pension Plan (QPP) (contributory). When the federal government intervenes by means of non-contributory assistance schemes such as OAS and GIS, it is probably not bound by the constraints of provincial predominance provided for in s.94A of the Constitution, since, as some writers claim, the constitutionality of these programs is linked to the federal spending power rather than to the jurisdiction conferred by s.94A.[126] Moreover, six provinces have added their own programs to the ones instituted by the federal government.[127]

The contributory schemes (CPP/QPP), which are based on s.94A of the Constitution, are more rigid. In fact, in order to secure provincial support for adding s.94A to constitutional texts, the federal government has accepted direct provincial participation in the administration of the Canada Pension Plan. Pursuant to this agreement, the *Canada Pension Plan Act* makes provision for a veto system by which the federal government or at least two-thirds of the provincial governments representing two-thirds of the Canadian population (including Quebec) must approve any amendment to the CPP.[128] Although Quebec administers its own pension plan, development of the QPP parallels that of the CPP. This high degree of coordination is the result of the desire of the participants to maintain an atmosphere that favours the free movement of individuals and capital; but it is also explained by the (formal) constraints imposed by the *Canada Pension Plan Act* — which requires any province exercising its right to withdraw to have a plan which provides benefits similar to those of the CPP — and by the (informal) constraints created by Quebec's right to intervene in any amendment to the CPP.[129]

## Provincial Powers

In spite of Parliament's broad authority to regulate the movement of capital, the provinces do have considerable latitude to intervene.

### Property, Civil Rights, and Matters of Local or Private Nature

Provincial jurisdiction over "Property and Civil Rights in the Province" and "generally all Matters of a merely local or private Nature in the Province"[130] is the basis of the legality of provincial regulations dealing with capital markets.

Long ago, the Privy Council established the basic criteria for distinguishing between provincial jurisdiction pursuant to s.92(13) (property and civil rights) and federal jurisdiction pursuant to s.91(2) (the regulation of trade and commerce). In *Citizens' Insurance Company of Canada v. Parsons*,[131] Sir Montague Smith limited the scope of s.91(2) to interprovincial or international commerce and to the general power of economic regulation, attributing local commerce to the provinces by virtue of s.92(13) of the *Constitution Act, 1867*.

Among other things, a province can require that a company that wants to operate in its territory must be registered with the provincial authority designated for that purpose. However, in the case of federally incorporated companies, this requirement must not infringe on the corporate powers of the company concerned. Most provinces require that foreign companies be registered, and it does not seem that the terms and conditions of registration have reduced the mobility of capital, even if they have been used to filter the establishment of companies.[132] In addition, in extreme cases, the provinces can monopolize a specific activity that is within their jurisdiction; for example, the nationalization of automobile insurance in some provinces.[133]

From the point of view of the movement of capital, provincial intervention is mainly manifested in the sectors of insurance, securities, financial intermediaries, pensions, and foreign investment.

#### INSURANCE

The right to regulate insurance, truly the private preserve of the provinces, has often been reaffirmed.[134] Provincial jurisdiction over insurance is by now so firmly anchored in Canadian constitutional law that it is reasonable to conclude that provincial intervention limiting the free movement of capital in this sector is constitutional. Several provinces have legislation which determines what proportion of their assets insurers under their jurisdiction must invest or must keep in Canada or within the territorial limits of a province; or legislation which provides for the composition of boards of directors, or even for control over direct investment by non-residents in the capital of such companies.[135]

Some experts feel that the constitutionality of the federal government's control over the insurance sector by virtue of the *Canadian and British Insurance Companies Act*,[136] the *Foreign Insurance Companies Act*,[137] and the *Department of Insurance Act*[138] is very precarious,[139] whether it is based on the commerce clause or on the power to legislate for peace, order, and good government; indeed, the insurance sector operates within a framework of provincial legislation and administrative formalities which have been carefully harmonized among the provinces.[140] Consequently, it is mainly through the federal government's legislative power over naturalization and aliens, over the incorporation of companies, and especially over insolvency that the federal authorities are able to exercise control in this area. We note, in fact, that despite the constitutional authority of the provinces, standards of solvency and the supervision of life insurance companies are, to a great extent, controlled by the federal superintendent of insurance.[141]

## SECURITIES

Since the famous case of *Lymburn v. Mayland*,[142] the courts have considered the field of securities as being under the legislative jurisdiction of the provinces. The courts do not hesitate to apply the double-aspect theory in support of the constitutionality and the opposability to third parties of provincial legislative provisions, considered under one aspect as relating to securities law, and of federal legislative provisions relating to the same subject but linked to parliamentary jurisdiction.[143] According to Professors Anisman and Hogg, this generosity is the result of the fear that there could be dishonest transactions if provincial measures were declared invalid in the absence of federal securities legislation to fill the void thus created.[144] On the other hand, a province cannot confer upon a provincial agency a discretionary power which allows it to prohibit the issue of securities by a federally incorporated company, since its capacity to raise capital is considered to be an essential attribute of corporate status.[145]

The provinces can require that federally incorporated companies use stockbrokers holding provincial licences in order to issue securities, and they can generally regulate securities transactions as such, as well as related businesses.[146] In its recent report on the participation of banks and other financial institutions in the trading of securities, the Ontario Securities Commission made the following recommendations:

Any person or company, but we expect that this will be of interest only to financial institutions, which wishes to offer a discount access must obtain the appropriate registration from the Commission.

The procedure for registering "order execution access dealers," which was subsequently established, prohibits such dealers from giving their clients financial advice.[147] The Securities Commission has even let it be known that a statement by the Canadian Parliament to the effect that such an activity would constitute "banking business" and would not diminish the power of the legislatures to control it.[148] The situation is similar in Quebec. The Quebec Securities Commission requires that financial institutions which want to participate actively in brokerage or in selling securities must register with the commission;[149] this requirement would seem legitimate, since the courts have held that such services do not constitute the "business of banking" (which seems obvious), which is subject to the exclusive jurisdiction of Parliament.

There have traditionally been three main aspects to the provincial regulation of securities: the communication to investors of relevant financial information; the registration of authorized professionals working in this area in order to ensure the integrity and quality of the services offered; and the definition of the penal and civil remedies available. In the past twenty years, interprovincial cooperation has increased considerably; the aim of standardizing measures imposed by the legislative or administrative authorities involved has gradually evolved toward a search for compatibility. Thus, despite the differences in requirements with respect to the continued disclosure of information, the provincial commissions have reached a high level of coordination, which has considerably reduced the costs associated with abiding by regulations for those who are subject to them. On the other hand, the processing of public offers on a multijurisdictional basis by issuing a securities prospectus may somehow get in the way of achieving optimum financial intermediation, in spite of exemplary interprovincial cooperation. Similarly, the diversity of approaches adopted by provincial regulators with respect to exemptions to the general regulatory scheme creates some confusion, which is contrary to the interests of investors.[150]

The most obvious problem raised by provincial jurisdiction is the territorial limitation of the application of securities legislation.[151] On several occasions, the courts have demonstrated their preference for maintaining the constitutionality of provincial legislation. In *R. v. MacKenzie Securities Ltd.*, a stockbroker registered in Ontario was found guilty of violating the Manitoba securities act for having solicited Manitoba clients by telephone and by mail without being licensed by that province to do so.[152] Previously, in *Gregory v. Quebec Securities Commission*, the Supreme Court had confirmed the applicability of the Quebec legislation to a Montreal company which was promoting, outside Quebec, shares in a mining company.[153] In spite of these decisions, the territorial limitations on the applicability of provincial legislation means that its effectiveness is doubtful, since it is relatively easy to circumvent by arranging to be subject to a more lenient regulation in another province. An example of this is the recent debate on the intention of the Ontario Securities Commission to punish extraterritorial violations of the provisions of the Ontario legislation dealing with take-overs (including the very controversial follow-up offer).[154]

As we have seen, the increasingly interprovincial or international nature of securities operations brings up the issue of maintaining provincial jurisdiction in this area, and it would not be surprising if the exclusiveness of provincial jurisdiction in this sector was reduced in the next few years.

## NEAR-BANKS

Credit unions and caisses populaires, trust companies, mortgage loan companies, and public-sector savings organizations are considered to be "near-banks."

### Credit Unions and Caisses Populaires

The creation and regulation of credit unions and caisses populaires comes under the jurisdiction of the provincial authorities by virtue of ss.92(11) and (13) of the *Constitution Act, 1867*, although many of their operations are identical to those of banks. In the case of *Caisse populaire Notre-Dame Limitée v. Moyen*, Mr. Justice Tucker of the Saskatchewan Court of Queen's Bench did, however, consider at length the relative weakness of provincial jurisdiction, which depends on the absence of incompatible provisions enacted by Parliament pursuant to its jurisdiction over banking.[155] Parliament's reluctance to assume regulatory control over credit unions and caisses populaires was demonstrated in the federal *Cooperative Credit Associations Act* and *Canadian Payments Association Act*, which recognize the existence of institutions incorporated under provincial legislation.[156] Finally, it is important to remember that the reason these institutions are regulated by the provinces is that at the beginning of the century the federal government felt that it did not have the power to regulate them itself.[157]

### Trust Companies and Mortgage Loan Companies

Trust companies are divided into those incorporated and regulated by the provinces and those incorporated and regulated by the federal government. In Ontario (as of November 1, 1983) there were 57 trust companies in operation; 20 of them were incorporated in Ontario and 12 in other provinces. The remainder were federally incorporated.[158]

Provincial jurisdiction over these institutions (except those that are federally incorporated) has been confirmed by the Manitoba Court of Appeal in *Re Bergethaler Waisemant*[159] and more recently by the Supreme Court of Canada in the case of *Canadian Pioneer Management Ltd.*

### Public-Sector Savings Organizations

In addition to private near-banks, the Canadian financial system includes savings organizations of modest size which belong to the provincial governments of Ontario and Alberta and are controlled by them. The Province of Ontario Savings Office can accept deposits from the Ontario public, but its lending power is limited:

> for the public service, for works carried on by commissioners on behalf of Ontario, for the covering of any debt of Ontario on open account, for paying any floating indebtedness of Ontario, and for the carrying on of the public works authorized by the Legislature.[160]

The Province of Alberta operates Treasury branches which are authorized to accept deposits from the public and to lend money. It was the constitutionality of provincial jurisdiction over this type of financial institution that was cited by the Manitoba Court of Queen's Bench in *Winnipeg Trustee v. Kenny* and by several judges of the Alberta Court of Appeal and the Supreme Court in the *Breckenridge* case.[161] However, the recent Supreme Court of Canada decision in the *Canadian Pioneer Management Ltd.* case gives reasonable grounds to believe that the validity of the provincial regulation of these institutions is a result of the absence of federal legislation enacted by Parliament by virtue of its jurisdiction over banks.

## OTHER FINANCIAL INTERMEDIARIES

The provinces, because of their jurisdiction over property and civil rights, have authority over mutual funds in the context of their securities legislation. It can be argued, however, that the international ramifications of the activities of this type of company could justify the predominance of federal legislation.[162]

Consumer finance companies obtain funds mainly by investing, in other financial institutions or corporations, securities that are issued for a period varying from 30 days to 3 years; they do not accept deposits from the public.[163] These companies include consumer loan companies, financial corporations, and commercial and industrial leasing companies. Their activities are largely regulated by the provinces, but federal intervention is evident from the existence of the *Investment Companies Act*, which applies only to federally incorporated companies.[164]

## PENSION PLANS

The Privy Council decision in *Reference re Unemployment Insurance*[165] opened the door to the provincial regulation of contributory and obligatory pension plans. The subsequent addition to the Constitution of s.94A, which gave Parliament the right to legislate with respect to old-age pensions and supplementary benefits, was not in theory intended to encroach upon provincial prerogatives, since the provinces maintained the principle of the primacy of their legislation in this area. In addition, their authority is reinforced, as far as provincial public officials are concerned, by s.92(4), which establishes their legislative jurisdiction over "the Appointment and Payment of Provincial Officers."

In 1963, Ontario enacted provisions to protect those participating in private professional pensions plans. Since then, the federal government and all of the provinces (except British Columbia and Prince Edward Island) have followed suit with similar regulations. However, this harmonization of the provincial and federal provisions regulating pension funds might not withstand[166] the pressures created by the increasingly obvious tensions (especially with respect to protection against inflation) regarding the period preceding the acquisition of the rights to devolution, to the improvement of transferability, and to increased protection for the spouse. Although the wording of s.94A expressly provides that the provincial legislation shall predominate, it does not seem that this would ultimately prevent Parliament or the courts from imposing a certain degree of uniformity on the basis of other areas of legislative competence, such as the commerce clause. Thus, protectionist and discriminatory provincial rules could be declared unconstitutional because of the fact that they would interfere unduly with interprovincial or international trade or commerce.

Although the Constitution allows the provinces to regulate pension plans, only Quebec has instituted a contributory and obligatory public pension plan, the Régime de rentes du Québec (Quebec Pension Plan), which is distinct from the Canada Pension Plan in which the other provinces participate. Although the two plans have evolved in a parallel manner since they were established, it is feared that they might go their own separate ways within the next few decades.[167]

## CONSUMER PROTECTION

### *Inequitable Transactions*

Since the provinces have the power to regulate contracts, they have naturally taken a vital role in enacting measures to protect the public. With respect to capital as such, this power extends to setting aside dispositions that impose reparatory measures and granting compensatory damages in cases of inequitable contracts. This power cannot, however, compromise Parliament's jurisdiction over banks, interest, or bankruptcy and insolvency.[168]

In fact, the federal and provincial authorities cooperate or overlap, depending on the circumstances, in their respective interventions. With respect to fraudulent commercial practices, six provinces have passed legislation, while the federal authorities concern themselves in particular with the propriety of advertising on the basis of the provisions of the *Combines Investigation Act*, which deals with false or misleading advertising. It would seem that the various participants have managed to coordinate their efforts effectively in this area.[169] With respect to the orderly payment of the debts of insolvent debtors, after the Supreme Court decision in *Reference re Validity of Orderly Payment of Debts Act, 1959 (Alta.)*,[170] Parliament promulgated Part X of the *Bankruptcy Act*, which authorizes the application of this part of the act to be delegated to any province which so desires. To date, six have chosen this route; a seventh (New Brunswick) has opted for a special arrangement with the federal government, while Quebec and Ontario administer their own programs.[171] In 1976, the federal government undertook a large-scale operation relating to consumer credit, the aim being to establish uniform standards with respect to personal loans, to reduce interest rates, and generally to rationalize the federal legislation. Since the bill with respect to borrowers' and depositors' protection[172] created dissatisfaction in the legislatures that already regulated these activities, it was finally abandoned. More recently, the federal government tried again, but in vain, when it tabled Bill C-36 (*An Act to amend the Interest Act*).[173] This bill dealt in particular with certain terms and conditions of mortgages on real property.

## Data Processing

Section 92(13) of the *Constitution Act, 1867* authorizes the legislatures to regulate the key elements of the collection, content, storage, and dissemination of information in order to protect the privacy of citizens (except in the case of data banks in Canadian banks or when such regulation would interfere with the basic activities of a communications system that comes under federal jurisdiction). This power includes setting ethical standards and prescribing penalties.[174]

## Foreign Investment

Provincial jurisdiction over private law relating to property has been firmly established. Thus, in *Walter v. A.-G. Alberta*,[175] a provincial law restricting the right to acquire land as community property was held to be valid. With respect to foreign investment as such, the case of *Morgan v. A.-G. Prince Edward Island* confirmed the constitutional validity of a law governing a non-resident's acquisition of real property located in the province. Mr. Justice Laskin, speaking for the Supreme Court, said that federal jurisdiction over aliens was not diminished by the fact that a provincial act established distinctions based on residence in the province,[176] as long as that act did not actually mention aliens or naturalized citizens in such a way as to restrict their general capacity. One can thus affirm that the provinces can regulate investments and transactions on property, with the exception of applicable international uses, should the need arise, in domestic law, as well as the relevant provisions of imperial treaties and international treaties which have been signed by the Canadian government and have been given effect by the legislatures. The provinces can also have a monopoly in a field of activity that comes within their jurisdiction, as is demonstrated by the implementation by certain provinces of public automobile insurance plans and the provision of public utility services by provincial Crown agents.

## Powers of Taxation

Legislatures may legislate with respect to "Direct Taxation within the Province in order to the Raising of a Revenue for Provincial Purposes"; and since the enactment of the *Constitution Act, 1982*, they may raise money by any mode or system of taxation in respect of non-renewable natural resources and forestry resources in the province, and in respect of the primary production therefrom.[177] The provinces exercise their powers of taxation mainly by means of income tax, retail sales tax, taxes on income from the exploitation of natural resources, land tax, business tax, tax on the paid-up capital of companies, and from succession duties (in Quebec). Provincial taxation, like federal taxation, cannot be used to introduce customs duties indirectly into the Canadian economic union or to regulate an area of economic activity within federal jurisdiction, such as banking regulation or interprovincial or international commerce.[178] It must also yield to fiscal immunity as provided for in s.125 of the *Constitution Act, 1867*.

The flexibility of the prerogatives of provincial taxation allows each province to structure a fiscal regime which it deems appropriate, without having to make it compatible with the regime of the federal government or of the other provinces, since the Canadian Constitution does not make formal provision for the harmonization of fiscal measures. Harmonization is the result of the need to ensure the free movement of manpower and capital by eliminating discriminatory fiscal measures by one government at the expense of the others.[179]

The Royal Commission of Inquiry on Dominion-Provincial Relations (Rowell-Sirois Commission) described the disastrous consequences of the "fiscal jungle" of the 1930s, which was the result of a lack of coordination in the fiscal legislation then in force.[180] Since that time, relative harmonization has been achieved through collection agreements;[181] however, Quebec set up its own personal income tax scheme

(British Columbia, Ontario, and Alberta have also considered doing so on several occasions),[182] and Ontario, Quebec, and Alberta apply their own measures with regard to corporate income tax. Since 1972, in the context of these same agreements, various provincial tax credits, which are administered by the federal government, have been created.[183] In 1979, however, the federal authorities rejected British Columbia's request, in the context of these two agreements, to administer two tax credits; the first was equal to 5 percent of the dividends received by a public commercial company which had its head office and principal administrative offices in British Columbia, and it would have benefited the citizens of that province; the second was in the form of a deduction from the income of a small-venture capital company. The federal government decided that such measures would create barriers to the free movement of capital between provinces and that, for this reason, they were incompatible with the spirit of the agreements binding the federal government and British Columbia.[184] Following these events, the federal minister of finance reaffirmed, before the special committee on federal-provincial fiscal arrangements, that the federal government was committed to the harmonious operation of the Canadian economic union, and he set three guidelines which the government intended to apply in administering tax collection agreements:

> First, the measure must be able to be administered reasonably effectively. Second, the measure must not significantly erode or have the potential to erode the essential harmony and uniformity of the federal and provincial income tax systems. Third, the measure must not jeopardize the efficient functioning of the Canadian economic union by the erection of income barriers to normal interprovincial investment flows.[185]

In 1982, however, British Columbia proposed a tax credit that was intended to stimulate residential construction. In spite of these guidelines, the federal government agreed to administer the scheme and the deduction solely for the purposes of provincial taxation.

Since Quebec does not participate in tax collection agreements, it has greater latitude. In 1979 it instituted a stock savings plan which allows individuals to deduct from their taxable income the amount (with a ceiling) used to buy, on the primary market, the voting common shares of certain companies with head offices in Quebec. This very popular scheme has contributed to the financial success of certain companies.[186] In the opinion of economist Thomas J. Courchene, this fiscal measure "amounts to a significant impediment to the free mobility of capital within the nation."[187]

With respect to corporate income tax, Quebec and Ontario (which operate their own plans) have established tax exemptions that are of benefit only to certain types of developing companies (Sodeq in Quebec and SBDC in Ontario). Alberta, in its 1984 white paper on an industrial and scientific strategy, demonstrated its firm intention to shape its corporate income tax in terms of its own development priorities.[188] Another problem is that Quebec and Ontario do not have the same definition of what constitutes "the principal establishment" of a company, for the purposes of revenue-sharing between the provinces in which a company operates, and this could start a trend toward multiple taxation. Finally, six provinces collect different taxes on the paid-up capital of companies.[189]

On the other hand, all provinces (except Alberta) collect a retail sales tax. On various occasions, Ontario and Quebec have adjusted their schemes to favour certain products that are manufactured locally (in Quebec, textiles, furniture, and shoes; in Ontario, automobiles). Retail sales tax has a very limited effect on the actual movement of capital, but it can be very effective in altering the flow of products.

In summary, the tax exemptions, allowances, or credits whose effect is to stimulate or orient economic development seem to be intra vires the powers of the legislatures, since they do not really constitute regulation of economic activities as such. In the opinion of the federal government, it is primarily provincial or federal fiscal measures that cause major distortions in the capital markets.[190]

## The Incorporation of Companies

Unlike Parliament, the provincial legislatures have the formal constitutional power to incorporate companies; their jurisdiction includes "the Incorporation of Companies with Provincial Objects." The stipulation "with Provincial Objects," contained in s.92(11), might give the impression that provincial incorporation imposes a functional restriction, but in fact the case law has allowed only the territorial test.[191] In the financial institutions sector, the constitutionality of provincially incorporated credit unions, caisses populaires, and trust companies seems now to be established.

By incorporating companies, the provinces control standards for the internal operation of companies, and they can usually establish their rights and powers in terms of their objectives. The Quebec *Act Respecting the Acquisition of Shares of Certain Mortgage Loan Companies* requires the prior authorization of the minister of finance before a major shareholder can acquire a share in a corporation that has been "incorporated under an act of Quebec to make loans secured by hypothec or hypothecary claim . . . and whose assets . . . are in excess of $100 million."[192] More recently, the Ontario legislature passed a special law authorizing the registrar designated pursuant to the *Loan and Trust Corporations Act* to take charge of and sell the assets of the Crown Trust Company, a company incorporated provincially under Ontario law.[193] Alberta company law requires that at least half of the members of a board of directors be Albertans and Canadian citizens, while in British Columbia at least one director must be resident in that province. In the insurance or trust sectors, several provinces keep a tight rein on the composition of boards of directors and on the transfer of property belonging to provincially incorporated companies.[194]

On the other hand, to the extent that the courts will accept it, provincially incorporated companies will be able to challenge federal legislation that infringes on their status and is likely to interfere with their basic corporate rights and powers, especially those relating to finance. Thus, at the time of the recent debate on the federal bill dealing with the ownership of the shares of certain companies (Bill S-31), the report of the Senate standing committee on legal and constitutional affairs raised the problem of the applicability of provisions relating to the shareholding transactions of provincially incorporated companies.[195]

During the 1930s the Rowell-Sirois Commission, while noting the plurality of methods of incorporation then used by the provinces, concluded that these regimes operated satisfactorily, and the commission did not feel that it was appropriate to recommend a more functional reallocation of this power between the two levels of government.[196] Since then, the terms and conditions of incorporation, and the company law enacted by each of the provinces and by the federal government, have to a great extent been harmonized through the impetus of the federal *Canada Business Corporations Act*, passed in 1975.[197]

## The Economic Benefit of the Development of Natural Resources

As a general rule, the provinces are considered to own the natural resources located within their territorial limits. This principle means that the provinces have legislative responsibility for the administration and sale of public lands and provincial woods and forests. In addition, s.92A, which was added to the Canadian Constitution in 1982, will certainly be used in future by provinces so that they may, at their pleasure, change the direction of the development and management of natural resources, both in the provincial public domain and in the private domain. In fact, the provinces have historically regulated the various phases of the exploration, development, and sale of their own natural resources, or of private-sector resources, by invoking their general right to legislate on "property and civil rights" and the right conferred on them by s.92(5) of the *Constitution Act, 1867*. Thus, s.92A of the Constitution clarifies these powers.

Provincial ownership of natural resources does not directly influence the movement of capital within the Canadian economy as a whole, but it does constitute a preferred tool for provincial governments in "accumulating" capital that is useful as support for investment policies, all of which is permitted under the fiscal immunity provided by s.125 of the Constitution.

## Various Powers

### SPENDING POWER

Provincial spending power is linked to the Crown's prerogative to spend, pursuant to ss.126 and 92(2) of the Constitution. The latter section confers the power of taxation on the provinces "in order to the Raising of a Revenue for Provincial Purposes." This expression does not limit their spending power since, according to Mr. Justice Duff of the Supreme Court of Canada in *Re Employment and Social Insurance Act*, it simply means "for the exclusive disposition of the legislature." A whole range of government measures based on this power, such as grants, financial guarantees, and preferential buying policies, can create movements of capital which would not otherwise occur in these markets.[198]

### BORROWING POWER

The provinces are vested with the right to legislate with respect to "the borrowing of Money on the sole Credit of the Province." The Rowell-Sirois Commission examined the use of the provincial borrowing power in considerable depth in the wake of the near-bankruptcy of certain western provinces after the ravages of the Depression of the 1930s. Its recommendation, which has since been forgotten, was that the federal government should assume full responsibility for provincial non-self-supporting debts (including those of provincial agencies and local governments), whose payment the province could not ensure and guarantee on their own account, and that the provinces should be permitted to make only redeemable loans in Canadian currency for developmental purposes of productive public works either directly on the sole credit of the concerned province or with the prior authorization of the finance commission (which was to be established to manage the Canadian public debt).[199] This suggestion, had it been implemented, would have placed draconian restrictions on the methods of financing that were available to the provinces. The problem of coordinating loans from foreign sources is not purely theoretical, as the Quebec minister of finance pointed out at the Federal-Provincial First Ministers' Conference in September 1980:

> Even federal countries which are considered lands of freedom from the business point of view, Germany, for example, do not venture so far into the chaos of foreign borrowing as we are permitted to go, where we operate literally without any type of mutual coordination; fortunately the stock-brokers coordinate us because, as a government, we don't seem to manage it [translation].[200]

# Summary

With respect to the free movement of capital within the Canadian economic union, the Constitution does not contain any provision limiting either Parliament or the provincial legislatures. Certain provisions of the *Canadian Charter of Rights and Freedoms* (ss. 6, 7 and 15) could alter this situation, but in the absence of a substantial body of case law, it would be difficult to speculate on the impact these sections might have on the movement of capital. Lacking any formal recognition, the movement of capital is subject to the legislative and administrative control of public authorities, each of which is limited in its actions only by the intrinsic limits of its jurisdiction.

The division of legislative powers under the Constitution gives the central government paramount control over the movement of capital. Indeed, monetary questions, matters related to interest, exchange rates, and the incorporation and regulation of banks all come under the jurisdiction of the federal authority, and the central government has full powers of taxation. These few predominant powers firmly establish Parliament's authority, which the courts have always confirmed at appropriate moments. To these powers is added an elaborate range of economic powers which, in varying degrees, are likely to be invoked in support of central government actions that affect the movement of capital directly or indirectly. Among the most important are spending power, borrowing power, control of interprovincial or international transportation and communications companies, the power to incorporate companies, and criminal law.

In addition, despite the ambiguity surrounding its interpretation, Parliament's power to legislate for the peace, order, and good government of Canada leaves us with the possibility of federal intervention in a field that has become a "national concern." In any case, in an emergency, Parliament would be in a position (except for the limitations imposed by the *Canadian Charter of Rights and Freedoms*, insofar as it applies) to control the movement of capital for a limited period of time. In addition, the commerce clause, s.91(2), could be used to exercise a stronger negative control over provincial powers, while the general power of economic regulation — to the extent that the Supreme Court has given it life (it has not had much impact since its jurisprudential creation) — would allow Parliament to gain some regulatory control in new areas of economic intervention. Consequently, the power to legislate for the peace, order, and good government of Canada, and the commerce clause create areas in which parliamentary intervention is justifiable (e.g., national securities legislation, control of foreign investment, competition, and perhaps coordination of federal-provincial borrowing on foreign markets), even though such intervention does not have an indisputable constitutional basis. The central government is also in a position to control if not prohibit (with the exception of the provisions of the *Canadian Charter of Rights and Freedoms*) investment in areas of activity which are under its jurisdiction by virtue of the Constitution.

The provinces also have important powers. Making use of their jurisdiction over property and civil rights in the province, they have completely or partially monopolized regulatory control of large para-banking institutions such as trust companies, mortgage loan companies, provincial savings institutions, credit unions, and caisses populaires. However, their regulatory activism is exercised under the shadow of a "floating charge," which is present in the form of a potential parliamentary declaration that federal banking legislation applies to such institutions. Another area of provincial intervention, the regulation of the securities market, assures the provinces of control over a key sector of capital markets. To date, provincial legislative activity does not seem to have unduly fragmented the operation of these markets. This is probably partly due to the influence of the market forces themselves and to the implicit threat of direct intervention by the federal government. A preferred sector, the regulation of the insurance industry, is firmly established as being under provincial tutelage.

The provincial authorities are in a position to control foreign investments even in a discriminatory fashion (while observing the provisions of the *Canadian Charter of Rights and Freedoms*), on the basis of their power to regulate property and civil rights; in extreme cases, they can even monopolize the right to carry on business in an area of economic activity within their jurisdiction. Finally, the provinces' power to spend, to borrow, and to tax gives them real flexibility in controlling and directing the flow of capital. The virtual explosion of provincial fiscal policies and the wealth of grants of all kinds are a remarkable testimony to this statement. Finally, the regulation of pension plans assures the provinces of a powerful hold over a large amount of capital, which has grown exponentially. The harmonization of provincial legislation does, however, show clear signs of running out of steam, which means that we could soon see evidence of local variations in the funding of such plans. It is possible that this phenomenon will place real constraints on the movement of capital, since the provinces probably have the power to impose, for example, obligatory local reinvestment ratios for funds collected, as is already the case for life insurance companies in several provinces (this being said with the reservation that the negative protection of the economic union, which is made possible by the commerce clause, could be used more vigorously in the future).

# Chapter 2

# The Free Movement of Capital
# and the Regulation of Financial Institutions

In the preceding chapter, we described and evaluated the respective powers of Parliament and the provincial legislatures, as well as the constitutional guarantees provided by the *Canadian Charter of Rights and Freedoms* which are likely to affect the movement of capital within the Canadian economic union. We particularly emphasized the predominance of Parliament's economic powers with regard to the formulation and implementation of a national monetary policy and to the establishment and regulation of the banking system. We also pointed out the constitutional fragility of the provincial regulation of near-banks on the basis of tests suggested by the Supreme Court, a court which has been manifestly reluctant to establish rigid criteria based on rather ephemeral economic theories. In certain respects, the Supreme Court has clearly indicated that it prefers to leave to Parliament the political decision of whether to subject such institutions to banking legislation, while affirming that such action would itself be subject to certain constitutional constraints. In addition, we demonstrated the solidity of provincial regulatory control over the insurance and securities sectors, and the quality of federal and provincial jurisdiction over public and private pension plans. In short, in sharing legislative jurisdiction over the regulation of financial intermediaries, Parliament and the provinces are forced to be partners.

In this chapter, we leave jurisdictional and constitutional considerations behind to examine the concrete issue of the movement of capital, concentrating on the sector of financial institutions as a model. We shall attempt to identify the distortions which regulation can cause in the movement of capital and, where necessary, we shall assess the effects of such distortions. Indeed, the current debate about the possible diversification, on a national scale, of the activities of financial institutions which are incorporated or regulated at both the federal and the provincial level brings up the controversial issue of control of financial institutions in the Canadian federal state.

## The Regulation of Financial Institutions

### Subjecting Deposit Institutions to Banking Legislation

For more than two decades, the regulation of the activities of deposit institutions has been the subject of doctrinal and political controversy. Historically, the arguments for submitting near-banks to the same controls as banks have centred around two issues: the claim that para-banking institutions may interfere with the management of monetary policy; and the need to guarantee better liquidity and solvency in order to ensure satisfactory protection for savings.

In 1964, the Royal Commission on Banking and Finance (Porter Commission) concluded from its analysis of financial markets that "federal banking legislation must cover all private financial institutions issuing banking liabilities," in other words "to those financial intermediaries issuing claims which may be transferred immediately or on short notice by cheques or on customers' orders."[201] Being pragmatic, the commission exempted government deposit institutions from this principle, "because their soundness is assured by their parent governments." It also exempted deposit institutions with fewer than 50 clients, institutions that lend to the general public "but whose only short-term liabilities are in the form of marketable paper not redeemable on demand or at short notice," and securities dealers and brokers who hold funds for their clients or borrow on a short-term basis. Credit unions and caisses populaires were added to this limited group, but "only if the provincial authorities effectively assume responsibility for supervising them." However, the central societies of these local institutions must, according to the Porter Commission,

> be integrated into the national banking system in order to bring the movement under the common monetary regulation, to encourage its continuing contact with the national authorities and to ensure that sound liquidity standards will be maintained throughout the system.[202]

In support of its position, the commission based itself on the character of "each institution's liabilities," in other words that "the banking function is generally taken to include the issuing of claims which serve as means of payment or as close substitutes for such money claims."[203] Without making the monetary function a causal argument of its recommendation, the Porter Commission, as the economist François-Albert Angers rightly pointed out, used it "as a logical standard in its definition of the meaning of banking institution subject to a single federal banking act [translation]."[204] In the same vein, the commission defined its objective with respect to cash reserves as being the devising of a system which protects the public and ensures responsiveness to monetary control but which is also simple, equitable and does not needlessly disrupt the institutions."[205] The commission suggested that all banking institutions should be required to maintain the same ratio of cash against their short-term liabilities in order to assure all institutions engaged in the same type of business equitable treatment in the face of monetary controls; and that all banking institutions should be required to place their reserves, other than till money in the Bank of Canada, since this would favour improved contacts and working arrangements between the Bank of Canada and the institutions now holding their cash elsewhere."[206] The commission's argument, to the effect that monetary policy and the liquidity of financial institutions means that near-banks must deposit part of their cash in the Bank of Canada, has been vigorously disputed by Quebec's Comité d'étude sur les institutions financières.[207]

In 1974 the governor of the Bank of Canada, noting the predominance of chartered banks in accepting public deposits and short-term credit, concluded:

> The absence of cash reserve requirements applicable to depositary institutions other than the chartered banks has never, to my knowledge, frustrated the effort of the Bank of Canada to bring about as sharp a curtailment of the pace of monetary expansion and as large an associated rise in short-term interest rates as we were prepared to contemplate in the circumstances of the time.[208]

The concern for ensuring public protection by establishing standards for reserves deposited with the central bank became somewhat less relevant to the debate on subjecting all deposit institutions to banking legislation in the wake of the creation, in 1967, of the Canada Deposit Insurance Corporation and the Régie de l'assurance-dépôts du Québec.[209] Also, the 1967 revision of banking legislation sanctioned the extension of the powers of chartered banks and direct competition with trust companies and caisses populaires, without, however, making the latter subject to banking legislation.

Another aspect of the issue of requiring near-banks to deposit reserves in the Bank of Canada came up in the 1976 federal white paper on Canadian banking legislation. Postulating that "one cannot have a good national system if there are differences in regulations or uncertainties engendered by a whole range of standards for solvency and control [translation]," the federal government concluded that all para-banking institutions should be subject to the same regime as the banks, with regard to both compensation and reserves in the Bank of Canada. It stated, however, that "in all other areas, provincially incorporated institutions [shall continue] to be regulated by their provincial acts of incorporation and [shall] come under provincial jurisdiction [translation]."[210]

The reasons given to justify the requirement that near-banks have cash reserves — compensation, liquidity, monetary policy, equity — were strongly contested by some of the institutions concerned.[211] The strong provincial opposition to the reserve requirement for provincial financial institutions is explained in part by the existence of the indirect advantages which the deposit of non-remunerated reserves in the Bank of Canada gives the federal government (to some extent, primary and secondary reserves amount to a tax on subject institutions).[212]

In its study of deposit institutions, the Economic Council of Canada noted that it did not appear that the reserve ratios imposed on banks were "indispensable to monetary control." However, the council recommended that "all deposit institutions be required to maintain the same cash reserves for demand deposits and advance notice deposits as well as for term deposits which can be redeemed within one hundred days [translation]." It added that the maintenance of such reserves should be a condition of direct access to the compensation system and to eligibility for deposit insurance. According to the institutions, the funds should be deposited in the Bank of Canada or in an approved depository. The council felt that it was impractical to require local caisses populaires or credit unions to maintain reserves in the Bank of Canada. It preferred to impose this requirement on the central banks. The council recommended, in principle, that there should be a different approach to regulating deposit institutions, in light of the division of legislative responsibility in a federal state.[213]

The Senate standing committee on banking, trade, and commerce concluded that although near-banks are not required to deposit reserves in the Bank of Canada, they are affected by the Bank of Canada's monetary policy because banks have a large proportion of total deposits in cash.[214] Finally, the House of Commons standing committee on finance, trade, and economic affairs recommended:

> Any such definition of the "business of banking" or "banking" should not be applied to credit unions, caisses populaires, or federally and provincially incorporated financial institutions and provincial treasury branches, as this could lead to a federal/provincial jurisdictional dispute regarding the operation of the financial institutions.[215]

It is clear that the *Banks and Banking Law Revision Act, 1980* has recognized this compromise, since only those institutions specifically mentioned in its appendices are subject to its requirements, especially the requirements with respect to reserves, a fact that was not particularly well received by bankers.[216]

The Supreme Court of Canada's decision in *Canadian Pioneer Management Ltd.* enters into this debate. By opting for the formal test and the institutional test, the Supreme Court has demonstrated that it prefers to leave to Parliament the task of evaluating the grounds which justify subjecting certain financial institutions to banking legislation. This approach clearly demonstrates that Canada's highest court is reluctant to define the concept of the "business of banking" with too much rigidity, on account of controversial economic theories which are likely to change with the times. Thus, the management of monetary policy and the security of depositors' funds are no longer such acute issues as they were at the time of the publication of the Porter Commission's report. On the other hand, the discernible fragmentation of institutional specialization among the various financial intermediaries is now creating new tensions.

## Property and the Diversification of the Activities of Financial Institutions

The fragmentation of the activities of financial institutions, which began in the United States, has very quickly caused controversy in Canadian financial circles. The federal government has responded by creating a joint government-industry advisory committee, responsible for conducting a thorough analysis of the methods of providing financial services.[217] At the provincial level, Ontario has established a task force to examine the tendency to integrate financial services and to examine the issue of controlling foreign or Canadian ownership of financial institutions, including the phenomenon of cross-ownership. Under the chairmanship of J. Stefan Dupré, the committee was to file an interim report by the end of 1984, containing recommendations that could be implemented immediately.[218] Fifteen years after the publication of the report of the Comité d'étude sur les institutions financières (Parizeau Report), which recommended diversification in the financial sector,[219] Quebec has firmly committed itself to the process of transforming its own financial institutions. The insurance industry has already felt the effects with the enactment of Bill 75 (*Act to amend the Act Respecting Insurance and Other Legislative Provisions*), and the Quebec minister of finance is determined to complete this reform before the end of 1985, as far as caisses populaires, caisses d'économies, and trust and loan companies are concerned.

At the heart of the debate are some fundamental considerations: the degree of concentration of financial activities in the hands of a few companies; the ownership of financial institutions (including the acceptance of foreign investment); conflict of interest in the case of diversified financial enterprises; conflict of purpose within each institution; the protection of clients and shareholders; the solvency of companies; the choice between an institutional and functional type of regulation; and the constraints caused by the division of powers between Parliament and the provincial legislatures.[220]

The division of functions between financial institutions according to the "four pillars" occurred either as a result of restrictions on ownership imposed on institutions or because of regulation of their particular activities. For institutions under federal jurisdiction, the Canadian government has, during the past 20 years, enacted a package of legislative provisions which ensure the "Canadian content" of boards of directors and which impose severe constraints on the ownership of their shares and on their investments. At the same time, the provinces have adopted similar measures to apply to their own financial institutions.

## CANADIAN BANKS AND THE BANK ACT

### Ownership

In 1967, following the sale of the Mercantile Bank of Canada to the First National City Bank of NewYork, and in view of British Columbia's significant shareholding position in the Bank of British Columbia, the principle which says that banks must not be controlled by a shareholder or a group of associated shareholders was incorporated into banking legislation.

These changes prevented any government from owning shares in banks, and they limited to 25 percent the proportion of such shares that could be owned by non-residents and limited to 10 percent the proportion that could be held by one individual (and, where applicable, by his associates), whether resident or not; residents were, however, authorized to exceed this limit in the case of a new bank. Finally, it was specified that at least three-quarters of the directors of any bank must be Canadian citizens and must normally be resident in Canada.[221]

The *Banks and Banking Law Revision Act, 1980* re-enacted the basic features of these provisions to Canadian banks (the banks mentioned in Schedule A of the act).[222] However, an important amendment was added to the new legislation. Henceforth, provincial governments were authorized, subject to the prior approval of the Governor in Council, to own voting shares of a new bank up to a maximum of 25 percent, with the obligation to reduce this percentage to 10 percent or less within ten years.[223] The same principle applies to financial institutions and to individual Canadians who want to start a new bank.[224] Finally, complementary provisions prohibited the exercise of voting rights that are attached to the shares of a bank held by a guarantee fund or pension fund to which the said bank is a contributor, or of any deemed association, for the purposes of banking legislation, between central cooperative credit societies, federations of cooperative credit societies, and local cooperative credit societies.[225]

### Diversification

The banking legislation provides that a bank may perform operations generally related to the "business of banking." The *Bank Act* formally lists a certain number of operations which banks are authorized to perform. With regard to services not expressly mentioned in the act but offered by a bank, it is up to the bank to show, if necessary, that these services come within the concept of the "business of banking."[226] However, banking legislation confirms the principle of a demarcation between banking activity, on the one hand, and trust, securities, and insurance activity[227] on the other hand.

After 1954, changes made to banking legislation allowed banks to offer mortgage loans covered by the *National Housing Act* and to accept chattel mortgages as guarantees for consumer loans. The revision of banking legislation in 1967 increased the penetration of Canadian banks into areas of activity that had previously been reserved for some of their competitors. The abolition of the 6 percent ceiling on debit interest rates for chartered banks allowed them to penetrate the consumer loan market.[228] As the economist Thomas J. Courchene has pointed out, eliminating credit ceilings helps to eliminate barriers to the free movement of capital in Canada.[229] In addition, the possibility of making ordinary mortgage loans, as well as those secured through the *National Housing Act*, has allowed banks to get more actively involved in the mortgage market, which had, up to that time, essentially remained in the hands of trust companies or mortgage loan companies and caisses populaires.

The 1980 reform expanded the chartered banks' areas of intervention by making formal provision for their right to act as agents in relation to accounts receivable (factoring services) and to offer financial leasing but only through subsidiaries, and it specified their powers in the computer field and in "quasi-trust" activities (mutual funds, retirement savings plans and home-ownership savings plans, real-estate investment trusts, and mortgage investment companies).[230]

In the field of securities, the 1976 white paper on the revision of banking legislation suggested that such legislation "instead of giving banks the general right to deal in securities, should specify the activities which they may and may not get involved in [translation]."[231] The *Banks and Banking Law Revision Act, 1980* gave effect to this principle by defining the powers of banks to intervene in this sector.[232] The Ontario Securities Commission provides a concise summary of the prerogatives of banks:

> It is fairly clear then that the Bank Act defines a number of activities with securities overtones as banking and the Securities Act generally accepts the definitions in the Bank Act by granting registration exemptions to the banks in respect of those activities. In summary, a bank (i) can only trade in the secondary market in equity securities on an unsolicited basis through registered brokers, (ii) can trade government debt securities without registration, (iii) is precluded from giving advice in respect of securities, except on a casual basis for no monetary consideration (an activity which also appears to be exempt from the adviser registration requirements of the Securities

Act), and (iv) is precluded from acting as an underwriter of corporate securities, but may act as a member of a selling group without registration under the Securities Act if its participation in the selling group is confined to filling orders from clients received on an unsolicited basis.[233]

In fact, the provisions of the *Bank Act* which deal with securities recognize the "four pillars" principle while respecting the predominant role of brokers to act as underwriters for securities. The recent controversy over the Toronto-Dominion Bank's establishment of its "Greenline Service" was not in itself a result of the 1980 amendments to banking legislation; rather, it was a result of the fact that the Ontario Securities Commission had eliminated fixed brokerage rates in order to liberalize brokerage fees. In reality, the brokers were afraid that this was only the beginning and that, sooner or later, the banks would demand the right to offer their clients better services with respect to securities.[234]

In conformity with the rule which says that banks should not engage in non-banking activities and that they should engage only in banking activities within the framework of their organization, the *Bank Act* provides that a bank may not hold shares amounting to more than 10 percent of all of the voting shares issued and outstanding of any Canadian company, including a loan company. The standard is strict with respect to investments in a trust or loan company, in a financial corporation which takes deposits, and in a company which is engaged in data processing. On the other hand, a bank may temporarily (for two years) exceed this limit in the case of other loan companies and other Canadian companies, or by being a silent partner in a limited partnership.[235] In addition, a bank may, wholly or in part, own shares in a bank service corporation or any Canadian corporation whose sole purpose is to finance exports; and subject to the terms and conditions set by the Governor in Council, it may own voting shares in a mortgage loan corporation, a venture capital corporation, a leasing or factoring corporation, or a corporation whose activities are limited to assisting in the establishment or operation of a real estate investment trust company or mortgage investment company. Finally, a bank may not acquire, deal in or lend money, or give advances, on the security of its own shares or those of another bank.[236]

## FOREIGN BANKS

### Foreign Banks in Canada

Banking legislation allows foreign banks to operate on Canadian territory through representative offices whose functions are purely passive or through subsidiaries (mentioned in Schedule B of the act).[237] Generally, a foreign bank cannot carry out banking operations in Canada, and it cannot set up branches or operate automated teller machines or other terminals from a remote service unit.[238] Provision has, however, been made for important exceptions. With the authorization of the Governor in Council and pursuant to the terms and conditions set by it, a foreign bank may set up a Canadian head office and carry out all "action reasonably necessary for the conduct of its banking activities abroad."A foreign bank may not own shares in a bank other than its own subsidiary, and it may not own more than 10 percent of the shares in any other federally or provincially incorporated commercial company that is involved *inter alia* in trust services, stock brokerage, or insurance.[239]

## Schedule B Banks

A subsidiary of a foreign bank may operate a branch in addition to its head office and, where appropriate, other branches approved by the minister of finance. In general, foreign banks have the same powers as Canadian banks, though they may not register share transfers in their securities register without the approval of the minister of finance, except in the case of a transfer of shares to the parent company. In addition, provincial governments may not invest in the share capital of Schedule B banks. These banks are restricted to a precise limit with respect to investments in real property and in one or more banking service companies. At least half of their directors must be Canadian citizens and must normally be resident in Canada. When a board of directors includes more than ten directors, committees of at least five directors may be created, and the majority of these directors must be Canadian citizens normally resident in Canada. The size and development of a subsidiary of a foreign bank is limited to twenty times its authorized capital or twenty times a lower amount established by the Governor in Council, except when the foreign bank chooses to Canadianize its subsidiary by selling its interest above 10 percent to Canadians.[240] Section 302(7) of the *Bank Act* limited to 8 percent the percentage of the overall amount of the average national assets which subsidiaries of foreign banks could own jointly; but in 1984, in response to the interest of Canadian banks in expanding into foreign markets, and subsequent to a favourable recommendation by the House of Commons standing committee on finance, trade, and economic affairs,[241] Parliament enacted Bill C-30 (*Bank Act Revision Act*) in order to raise to 16 percent the portion of these assets accessible to subsidiaries of foreign banks.[242]

## Trust and Loan Companies

In the 1960s, the *Trust Companies Act*[243] and the *Loan Companies Act*[244] were amended in order to limit to 10 percent the proportion of shares which could be transferred or issued to a non-resident (and associates); the total interest by a non-resident in a given company was limited to 25 percent. In both cases, at least three-quarters of the directors of the company had to be Canadian citizens normally resident in Canada.[245]

Ontario, Manitoba, and Alberta followed suit and established similar standards for provincially incorporated loan or trust companies.[246] Most of the other provinces have made provision for the composition of the boards of such companies or have demonstrated their willingness to impose local control through rules for registration which foreign companies must submit to if they want to do business on their territory.[247]

Some trust and loan companies have asked, over the years, for amendments to their articles in order to limit the voting rights provided for in their charters (e.g., Royal Trust, Nova Scotia Savings and Loans Company). In 1970, the *Trust Companies Act* and the *Loan Companies Act* were amended in order to allow trust companies to impose limits on voting rights and on the levels of participation by shareholders (with the proviso that any change must be approved by the minister of finance).[248]

Provincial governments have intervened much more vigorously during the past few years. In 1978, Quebec blocked the takeover of Crédit Foncier by enacting a law of general application, the *Act Respecting the Acquisition of Shares of Certain Mortgage Loan Companies*, which subjected to the approval of the minister of finance the acquisition of any Quebec company empowered to to make loans secured by hypothec or hypothecary claim and whose assets exceed $100 million.[249] Because of the acute problems of some trust companies, Ontario has, since December 1982, required the prior approval of the registrar, acting pursuant to the *Loan and Trust Corporations Act*,[250] for any transfer of voting shares from an Ontario trust or loan company which brings to more than 10 percent the total of shares held by a shareholder (and his associates). The debate at both federal and provincial levels has now shifted, using the principle established in the *Bank Act*, to a ceiling of 10 percent of the total shares which a shareholder (and his associates) would be permitted to own. The federal Liberal government advocated such a measure with respect to companies having deposit liabilities of $1 billion or more, whereas the Progressive Conservative government seems to favour establishing more stringent controls of self-dealing transactions in lieu of imposing a 10 percent ceiling on the ownership of non-banking financial institutions.[251] The Ontario government also seems to prefer to exercise stricter control over securities transactions, rather than enacting a rigid standard[252] for companies under its jurisdiction.

With regard to the investments of trust companies, the legislation establishes different limits in order to ensure that such companies have a well-balanced portfolio. With respect to direct investment, both the federal government and the Ontario government intend to reduce, from 30 to 10 percent, the proportion of common shares which a loan or trust company may acquire in any other company (except for certain types of subsidiaries which are engaged in accessory activities, as well as temporary investment in a venture capital company).[253]

When the 1982 white paper on the revision of the *Trust Companies Act* and the *Loan Companies Act* was published, the federal government of the time intended to standardize activities related to savings in federally incorporated companies in order to make it "substantially the same as that applying to banks." The policy statement did not question the federal government's prediction for separating the "four pillars." In fact, the federal authorities readily suggested a limit of 15 percent of the assets of a company subject to the proposed Canada Savings Banks and Trust Companies Act for commercial loans (including financial leasing but excluding mortgages), specifying that "it seems necessary to put a limit on this kind of activity if companies under this new legislation are to be distinguished from banks under the *Bank Act*." The federal government also weighed the possibility of eliminating a test of quality (requiring a historical account of dividends paid, etc.) and replacing it with general quantitative rules which would apply to the composition of the portfolio to ensure that it was diversified. The recent publication of a green paper on the regulation of financial institutions has confirmed the new (Progressive Conservative) federal government's willingness to undertake, in this same direction, a reform of the legislation that applies to federally incorporated trust companies.[254]

During the past few years, trust companies have substantially reduced the proportion of their mortgage loans in favour of commercial loans. In addition, federally or provincially incorporated trust companies are permitted to offer brokerage services in securities. Recently, the Quebec Securities Commission gave Fiducie du Québec (a provincial trust company associated with the Mouvement Desjardins) and the Royal Trust Company (a provincial trust company) restricted activity registration confirming their right to act as restricted practice brokers. Originally, authorizations stipulated that the dealer responsible for carrying out an operation must make sure that its clients' orders were for securities traded on the Montreal Stock Exchange or were executed on that exchange, "unless it is possible to obtain a more advantageous rate on another exchange." This condition was, however, removed soon afterwards.[255] National Trust, General Trust of Canada, and Canada Trust have also been authorized to act as restricted practice brokers.[256]

Ontario has suggested, in its white paper on the revision of trust and loan company legislation, a standard of 15 percent for commercial loans (to which we must add the freedom conferred by the omnibus clause, or 7 percent), similar to that suggested in the federal white paper. However, the Ontario white paper contains an important jurisdictional requirement in the sector of trust and loan companies, since Ontario wants to subject to its legislation all companies operating in its territory, whatever the statutory authority for their incorporation. At the outset, the white paper reluctantly admits that it is constitutionally difficult to reach federal and extraprovincial companies which control more than 80 percent of the assets and deposits in this sector in Ontario.[257]

## Life Insurance Companies

Federally incorporated life insurance companies are subject to standards of "Canadian content," which require that non-residents may not own, in total, more than 25 percent of of a company's shares and that any individual non-resident (and his associates) may not own more than 10 percent. In addition, a majority of the directors must be Canadian citizens who are normally resident in Canada.[258] Any foreign insurance company operating in Canada must, at all times, by virtue of the *Foreign Insurance Companies Act*, maintain in Canada, under the control of a Canadian trustee or the Receiver General of Canada, assets at least equal to its commitments to its insurees in Canada.[259]

As for provincially incorporated companies, British Columbia, Ontario, Saskatchewan, and Alberta, for example, require that a majority of the directors be residents of the province or of Canada.[260] Moreover, s.120 of the British Columbia *Insurance Act* prohibits any insurance company incorporated in BritishColumbia from being sold without the permission of the minister responsible; in Manitoba, the sale of an insurance company incorporated in that province is subject to the approval of the Lieutenant-Governor in Council.[261] Quebec has also established restrictions on the sale, to non-residents of Canada, of voting shares of insurance companies incorporated under its legislation, requiring that at least three-quarters of the directors be Canadian citizens and that a majority of them be resident in Quebec. In addition, the minister of finance has the authority to prohibit — or to authorize, on conditions which he will determine — any transfer or allotment of voting shares "entailing an increase of 10 percent or more in the number of such shares or to permit the registration of a transfer of such shares involving 10 percent or more of the issued shares or to every allotment or transfer of shares having the effect of increasing to more than 50 percent the number of such shares held by the same person."[262]

As is the case with trust companies, insurance companies are required to meet specific standards with respect to the distribution of their investments. In spite of these restrictions, some have undertaken to expand their activities to sectors which, until now, have been exclusively occupied by other institutions. Provincially incorporated companies, in association with trust companies, through financial holding companies, have become involved in the securities trade and in commercial loans.[263] The Canadian Life and Health Insurance Association is pressing the federal government to modernize and rationalize the legislation which applies to its members so as to give them the right to diversify "in any lawful business" by means of subsidiaries, up to a limit of 15 percent of the value of their assets. This association is opposed to reducing, from 30 to 10 percent, the proportion of voting shares which its members are authorized to own in a given company.[264]

The diversity of measures dealing with investments means that provincial legislation can alleviate the alleged rigidity of federal legislation. Thus, the Quebec legislation on insurance enables insurance companies incorporated in Quebec to create certain types of subsidiaries which federal legislation prohibits for federally incorporated companies. For example, any Quebec company may acquire a federally incorporated life insurance company as a subsidiary, although the converse is not permitted. In addition, Bill 75 (*An Act to amend the Act Respecting Insurance*),[265] which has been the subject of much discussion, is an important first step in diversifying the activities of financial institutions incorporated in Quebec.

Bill 75 gives life and health insurance companies and general insurance companies the right to carry out certain activities foreign to insurance, including managing immovables, leasing, offering for sale the products of a financial institution, offering custodial and safekeeping services, financing insurance premiums and annuity contributions and in general offering for distribution the products of a financial institution. This bill thus paves the way for insurance companies which want to get involved in offering products as varied as deposit certificates, chequing accounts, and securities.In the wake of these amendments, the Quebec Securities Commission held public hearings (in October 1984) on the effects of proposed dual registration of persons operating in the field of securities and insurance. In addition, the minister of finance can unilaterally authorize an insurance company to engage in "another activity" and can require the insurer to incorporate a subsidiary in order to carry out an activity (other than insurance) which represents more than 2 percent of his gross revenues.[266]

As far as investments are concerned, the bill reverses traditional procedure by eliminating objective standards on the quality of investments and substituting for them the diffuse requirement that the insurer should invest its funds like a "prudent and reasonable person and act with honesty and loyalty" in the best interests of the insured, the shareholders or, where applicable, the members of a mutual fund. With regard to quantitative standards, the bill establishes general ceilings, for the allocation of assets which are higher than those that other regulatory bodies accept. In addition, any insurer (other than a mutual fund) is authorized (within the limits of the ceilings mentioned in the act) to invest in any type of subsidiary and especially in other financial institutions or holding companies. As far as the ownership of insurance companies is concerned, the Quebec legislature has refused to insert the maximum standard of 10 percent of voting shares which a shareholder may own (alone or with his associates). Finally, companies which were not incorporated in Quebec but which are authorized to carry on business in the province have the same rights as Quebec insurance companies or Quebec mutual associations, except that they must respect the laws of the territory where they were incorporated if they are more restrictive.[267]

## THE SECURITIES SECTOR

The securities sector has been very much influenced by the dynamics of the diversification and pressures related to the control of the ownership of financial institutions, as is clear from the astonishing growth of "free credit balances" managed by brokerage firms and by current account management services, including privileges similar to the chequing accounts which some of them offer.[268]

From the beginning of the 1970s, Ontario limited to an overall maximum of 25 percent and to an individual ceiling of 10 percent the rate of participation by non-residents of Canada in the ownership of brokerage firms registered with the Ontario Securities Commission.[269] Self-regulating bodies followed the Ontario lead and have incorporated similar measures applying to their members into their internal regulation.[270] On the other hand, following the Parizeau, Bouchard, and Tetley reports, Quebec adopted an open-door policy with respect to foreign investment in this sector, preferring to exert minimal local control over participants.[271] The Quebec Securities Commission supported this policy by reversing the decisions of the Montreal Stock Exchange that were prejudicial to foreign investors and by prohibiting any restriction of this type which related to public brokerage firms registered in Quebec.[272]

Domestically, with regard to public ownership of brokerage firms, the Ontario measures provide that no one (other than a industry investor) may own, without the prior approval of the Ontario Securities Commission and the self-regulating bodies concerned, more than 10 percent of all of the voting rights attached to the issued and outstanding securities of a brokerage firm that is a member of one or other of these organizations. In addition, at least 40 percent of the directors of such a firm must be members.[273]

The debate on the ownership of brokerage firms is part of the much larger issue of the diversification of financial activities. In 1976, a joint committee of the securities industry took the view that stockbrokers and investment dealers should not get involved in the activities of banking, trust, loan, or life insurance companies (collectively known as "restricted companies"). On the other hand, the committee felt that these companies' diversification into non-financial activities would be acceptable only to the extent where such penetration would be carried out through separate companies and where it would not harm brokerage activities. In 1977, the Toronto Stock Exchange adopted the committee's recommendations and required that it be given prior notice of its members' plans for diversification.[274]

At the time of the public hearings held in 1982, the Ontario Securities Commission waffled over the issue of diversification. It reiterated its preference for the "four pillars" theory, and a majority of the commissioners concluded that restricted companies should not be allowed to have a direct or indirect interest in the property of a dealer or in a holding company that controls such a dealer. On the other hand, this same majority was opposed to the idea that dealers should be able to invest directly or through affiliated companies in the share capital of restricted companies. In 1982, while waiting for its recommendations with respect to the ownership of institutions to be approved by the competent authorities, the commission decreed a moratorium upon which it based its refusal to approve any participation above 10 percent by a restricted company in a member brokerage firm of either the Toronto Stock Exchange or the Investment Dealers Association of Canada. With respect to diversification by networking, by which the dealers become preferred agents of restricted companies for certain types of operation, the commission demonstrated caution in accepting the principle, subject to prior approval in each case by the commission itself, by the superintendent of loan and trust companies, and by the independent regulatory associations involved.[275]

The whole question soon resurfaced, however, when Daly Gordon (now Gordon Capital) announced its intention to create, in equal partnership with the Belgian company Lambert-Brussels Corp., a company whose mandate was to operate on markets that were not subject to the control of the Ontario Securities Commission, including those pertaining to foreign investment. The self-regulating bodies (the Toronto Stock Exchange and the Investment Dealers Association of Canada) exercised their right to veto this project; the Ontario Securities Commission then organized new public hearings (in November and December 1984), this time to study not only the regulation of ownership in the context of foreign investment and Canadian investment but also the advisability of maintaining exemptions from registration with the commission.[276] The commission, noting the changes that had occurred in the financial markets, recommended in its report, which was made public in February 1985, a restructuring of the existing regulatory framework on the basis of two premises: the maintenance of a significant degree of Canadian ownership of securities firms; and respect for the segregation of the activities of the various institutions which make up the Canadian financial system according to the "four pillars" guidelines.[277]

With respect to ownership, non-resident as well as financial institutions (including on an individual basis) would be permitted to own up to a maximum of 30 percent of the voting rights or equity participation of a brokerage firm registered with the Ontario Securities Commission. On the other hand, investors (other than industry investors and those who were neither non-residents nor financial institutions) would be permitted joint ownership of up to 49 percent of the participating or voting shares of such a brokerage firm, though each investor would be restricted to a ceiling of 30 percent. In addition, in all of the cases described above, an industry investor would be required to control at least 51 percent of the voting rights or equity participation of the dealer registrant as soon as the investments — whether by non-residents, financial institutions, or resident investors other than industry investors — together exceeded 10 percent of the participating or voting shares of that firm.[278]

Instead of raising the ceilings for investment by authorized non-residents, the Ontario Securities Commission recommended that brokerage firms who wanted to do business in Ontario and whose participating securities were more than 30 percent owned by non-residents should be required to register with the commission as a "foreign dealer registrant." The maximum aggregate of the capital of brokerage firms subject to such conditions would be 30 percent of the whole securities industry.[279] In addition, each of them would be limited to a maximum of 1.5 percent of the total capital of the industry. Finally, the selection and number of brokerage firms authorized to operate in this capacity would be at the discretion of the commission. Brokerage firms controlled by non-residents would, however, be exempt from the obligation to register if their operations in Ontario were limited to activities which facilitated the financing of Canadian issuers outside Ontario or which allowed Canadian investors to deal in securities outside the province.[280]

In fact, for the first time, the Ontario Securities Commission has suggested extending its regulatory power to numerous financial transactions which are subject to a scheme exempt from OSC's controls.[281] Thus, there will be demands for eliminating registration exemptions for private investments, as well as those given to certain financial institutions and certain purchasers. Consequently, the private subscription of securities as well as the provision of brokerage services will be permissible only through persons duly authorized by the commission.[282] Finally, the commission has said that brokerage firms may distribute financial products of other financial institutions, provided that the prior approval of the director of the commission is given in each case.[283]

On the other hand, several months before the Ontario Securities Commission published its 1983 report on the ownership and diversification of brokerage firms, the Quebec Securities Commission had already opted for diametrically opposite solutions to the same problems. On the basis of the principle that "free competition constitutes one of the basic postulates of our economic system," the Quebec Securities Commission said that "artificial barriers to the ownership of companies in a particular sector are justified only in circumstances when the normal rules of competition are deficient and put the public interest at risk." Thus, the Quebec commission affirmed its intention not to oppose takeovers or the strengthening of a strong position (in other words, more than 10 percent of the voting shares) in a brokerage firm by anyone (including a restricted company) "unless there are specific grounds for believing that this transaction is contrary to the public interest or that the future shareholder does not meet the tests of integrity, competence and solvency required by the Act." In the same spirit of free competition, the commission expressed the opinion that it was not appropriate arbitrarily to prohibit a dealer "from exercising activities other than those which he would traditionally exercise or from buying voting securities with the voting rights of a person exercising another activity including a financial activity [translation]," to the extent that everything is carried out by an intermediary acting on behalf of one or more distinct legal entities.[284]

## CAISSES POPULAIRES AND CREDIT UNIONS

Quebec caisses populaires are very much involved in diversifying their activities. Thus, the Mouvement Desjardins has founded or acquired various institutions and companies in the fields of general insurance (Le Groupe Desjardins, Assurances générales), life insurance (Assurance-vie Desjardins and La Sauvegarde, compagnie d'assurance sur la vie), trust and securities services (Fiducie du Québec), investment (La Société d'investissement Desjardins), and the financing of commercial companies (Crédit industriel Desjardins Inc.). In addition, the Quebec minister of finance is already committed to modernizing the applicable legislation in order to sanction the expansion and diversification of the group's activities. Finally, in September 1984 the Quebec Securities Commission granted an exemption to any caisse populaire that wanted to advertise securities eligible under the Quebec stocks savings plan, in the context of a dividend re-investment plan or a stock subscription plan, and on the services offered by the Fiducie du Québec.[285] The institutions which are members of the Canadian Cooperative Credit Society want to expand their powers considerably, especially with regard to commercial and international loans, liquidity ratios, and borrowing ratios.[286]

## FUNCTIONAL REGULATION

Because of the effects of reduction or maturity in some financial sectors, because of the size of financial institutions, and because of modern technology and government policies, competition intensifies and exacerbates tensions between the various institutions that are subject to distinct legislative and regulatory provisions. In its examination of deposit institutions, the Economic Council of Canada recommended a functional approach to the regulation of financial institutions in such circumstances.[287]

A functional rather than an institutional approach to regulation raises the specific problem of accommodating the legislative powers of Parliament and the provincial legislatures. In the case of *Canadian Pioneer Management Ltd.*, the Supreme Court relied on the formal and institutional test rather than on the functional test in dividing the respective responsibilities of Parliament and the provinces. In order to introduce functional regulation, a very high degree of federal-provincial cooperation will be necessary; otherwise there is likely to be a shift toward a national regulatory structure of all financial institutions.[288] In addition, the implementation of a functional system of regulation would probably mean that institutions performing the same operations would have to submit to the same obligations; for example, institutions that accept deposits from the public and offer chequing account services would be required to deposit reserves in the Bank of Canada.[289]

The federal government has now set up a joint advisory committee which includes representatives from the federal government and from industry (initially the MacLaren Committee); but the provinces have not been asked to join it, a fact that offended the Quebec minister of finance, Jacques Parizeau, to the consternation of critics of his program to diversify Quebec financial institutions.[290] In the wake of the work of the committee, the minister of state for finance, Barbara McDougall, was expected to present, in April 1985, the outline for an in-depth reform of the system for regulating the financial institutions sector. In a bold statement the federal government has proposed increasing competition between financial institutions, improving user services, and making financial markets more efficient by allowing banking institutions (future banks in Schedule C) and non-banking institutions to come together under the umbrella of a financial holding company.

As far as the government is concerned, the new legislation will present no barrier to the use of the ordinary distribution and marketing systems that are subject to provincial regulations and requirements with regard to licences. However, in order to facilitate surveillance, to assess the liquidity of financial institutions and the application of deposit insurance, the said institutions and financial holding companies would remain distinct legal entities. In addition, holding companies would be subject to the same provisions for the restriction of foreign ownership as those that exist in legislation with respect to trust and insurance companies, while the future banks listed in Schedule C would be subject to the same restrictions as those in Schedule A. Increased competition in the field of commercial loans would therefore be achieved through investment companies rather than by expanding the commercial lending powers of trust companies and other non-banking institutions. In addition, the federal government's green paper recommends a tightening of control over self-dealing transactions, as well as over those that involve conflict of interest, and a restructuring of the supervision of all financial institutions by the creation of a new administrative agency.[291]

The absence of uniformity in federal regulatory measures and provincial measures is a result of the very dynamics of the specific aims of each of these levels of government. According to Professors Chant and Dean, the federal and provincial authorities respond to market forces in different ways, according to their different assessments of the costs and the benefits of regulating financial institutions. Thus, the provincial regulatory authority is particularly sensitive to the transfer, through spillover, of the advantages of its regulation outside its territory. In addition, the provinces are naturally inclined to want to reduce the costs of federal regulation while maintaining the benefits for their citizens. Finally, the peculiarities of the financial markets and of the institutions which serve them sometimes explain the reasons for an apparent normative discrepancy. Thus, in the insurance sector, it is clear that the Quebec legislation reflects the maturity and size of the financial institutions involved.[292]

## Technology and the Payments System

Technological developments profoundly alter the methods of payment in Canada. Automated teller machines are in use throughout Canada and their number is rapidly increasing; direct transfers and pre-authorized debits are also increasing rapidly. Debit cards will probably make their appearance by 1987.[293] Interbank payment is moving resolutely toward computerization under the auspices of the Canadian Payments Association, whose mandate specifically includes a plan to develop "a national payments system."[294] The legal and constitutional problems accompanying these changes have been the subject of many studies, which point out the necessity of modernizing the relevant legislation.[295]

The Canadian payments system is now governed by the *Bank of Canada Act*, which provides that the central bank is the reserve bank and the final payment bank for deposit institutions; by the *Bills of Exchange Act*, which provides for the rights and privileges of parties to bills of exchange or cheques; and by the *Canadian Payments Association Act*, which establishes the terms and conditions of compensation between member institutions.[296] It is possible that Parliament could enact legislation on electronic transfers (similar to the American *Electronic Fund Transfer Act*), because of its jurisdiction over banks and currency.[297] Similarly, it is possible that the provinces have the power to legislate to protect those using automated payments systems, with respect to deposit institutions within provincial jurisdiction.[298]

It therefore seems unlikely that the movement of capital will suffer very much as a result of the duality of federal and provincial legislation.

Current indecision is the result of the absence of existing regulation, rather than the result of a conflicting overlap between the two levels of government.

## Securities Transactions

We have already discussed the doctrinal work carried out by a federal task force during the 1970s with the intention of working out a federal securities legislation. The reasons given for enacting such legislation are the national and international character of the market, increased automation in the Canadian stock exchange network, the assumed inability of provincial bodies to provide harmonious regulation of operations which overreach their respective territories (as well as the desire to standardize measures), and the strong competition of the American stock market. The federal plan to create national securities legislation was not at all well received by the provinces.[299] Consequently, the federal authorities have adopted a wait-and-see attitude, preferring to avoid controversy.

The joint Senate and House of Commons committee suggested in 1972 that the regulation of stocks and securities should come under "common jurisdiction with the federal Parliament prevailing [translation]," affirming that the absence of uniformity of legislation from one province to another amounted to "a lack of protection for the investor [translation]."[300] This statement seems to be an exaggeration, judging from the Canadian Bar Association's description of the provinces' exercise of their authority in these matters. The bar association was also very hesitant about the prospects of concurrent regulation, since such a situation could be harmful "to shareholders and to entrepreneurs since they would have to take two regulations and two administrations into account [translation]." In spite of the problems related to provincial regulation of the securities market, the bar association concluded that the latter "should generally come under provincial jurisdiction"; measures to protect the public would not create direct barriers to the movement of capital, since their purpose would simply be to help investors make a choice.[301]

## Institutional Investors

Intervention by financial institutions that invest in companies' shares and debt securities, and in public-sector debts is clearly increasing. Since several years ago, trading by individuals has represented only 49 percent of the total value of trading on the Toronto Stock Exchange; shares held by pension funds alone represented (at the end of 1976) 15 percent of the stock market value of Canadian shares quoted on that exchange.[302] According to a recent study prepared for the Business

Committee on Pension Policy, the assets of pension funds at the end of 1981 represented some $137 billion, and the rate of accumulation reached 23 percent of the gross annual savings in Canada, as against 12 percent at the beginning of the 1960s.[303] Large financial institutions have significant investments in common stocks, particularly the Caisse de dépôt et placement du Québec, the Alberta Heritage Savings Trust Fund, pensions plans held in trust, and insurance companies.[304]

Such activity by investors who specialize in the investment in participating securities prompts the statement that there are actually two levels to the financial market, the first being made up of shares in companies favoured by institutional investors, and the second consisting of other securities which do not enjoy this support.[305] However, this phenomenon does not seem to have interfered with the effective operation of financial intermediation. Indeed, using the test proposed by the Business Committee on Pension Policy (which says that owning more than 10 percent of all the shares or bonds on the markets would give its owner a dominant position), we note that there is now no institution in such a position. Undoubtedly, the anticipated increase in public pension funds could mean that one of them will exceed the above-mentioned limit. However, neither the federal government plan nor the Ontario government plan[306] includes the expansion of public pension funds; the intention is, rather, to use tax deductions to encourage individuals to save. (Quebec's position remains vague in this regard.) We can expect that the money thus channelled into private pension funds will be divided among numerous financial institutions, and this will reduce the risk of one of them acquiring a dominant position on the stock or bond market. The only apparent distortion affecting the efficient allocation of capital with respect to pension funds is a result not of their relative importance on the financial markets but of investment restrictions imposed upon them in the various segments of these markets ("market avoidance"). The Economic Council of Canada has also demonstrated its preference for an increase in investment in public pension investment through financial markets.[307]

The issue of institutional investors — pension funds, life insurance companies, trust companies — controlling commercial companies remains in dispute. The federal government is considering lowering, from 30 to 10 percent, the proportion of share capital which a loan, trust, or life insurance company can own in a commercial company, (except in certain specific cases), and Ontario seems to favour applying such a restriction to the loan and trust companies under its jurisdiction. In addition, certain interest groups hope that a 10 percent ceiling will be placed on voting rights held by public institutions (such as the large public-sector banks).[308]

In general, the provincial and federal legislatures have taken the view that being the owner of 10 percent of the voting shares of a company makes one an insider, and that anyone who owns 20 percent of such shares is in a position of control. According to a survey published by the Montreal Stock Exchange in 1982, only 22 of the 400 largest Canadian commercial companies did not have at least one shareholder holding 20 percent or more of their voting shares. Of the others, 187 were controlled by foreigners, 145 by individual Canadians, 17 by cooperatives, and 29 by governments. Being in a position of control is therefore the norm in Canada and diffused ownership is the exception, although large Canadian companies (Canadian Pacific, Bell Canada, Alcan) are in this category.[309]

The behaviour of institutional investors in their capacity as shareholders is very controversial. Should they or should they not be deprived, completely or partially, of the voting rights attached to their shares? To what extent should they be permitted to interfere in the management of the companies which they control? Should there be different standards for private institutional investors and for public investors such as the Caisse de dépôt et placement du Québec and the Alberta Heritage Savings Trust Fund? Most of these institutions are deemed to act as a "trust bond," in other words to find the most appropriate and most prudent profit-risk combination in order to honour their commitments to their depositors. To the extent that they act as trust bonds, it does not seem that there are any objective reasons (aside from the independence of the companies) to prevent them from acquiring a dominant position in a given company. In fact, some claim that it is unfair to deprive an institutional investor of the voting rights attached to its shares, since such rights are one of the best means of protecting money invested.[310]

The experience of the past few years has created certain doubts about the appropriateness of giving public institutional investors (e.g., Caisse de dépôt et placement du Québec and the Alberta Heritage Savings Trust Fund) the double mandate of honouring their trust bond obligations and encouraging economic development in their province. Some groups which appeared before the Royal Commission on the Economic Union and Development Prospects for Canada demonstrated their strong opposition to the continued expansion of public banks or, at the very least, their concern over these institution's investment policies.[311]

The Caisse de dépôt et placement du Québec's act of incorporation authorizes it to invest up to a maximum of 30 percent of its total assets in the common shares of companies, and it sets at 30 percent the ceiling on investment in the common share capital of any company. The act also contains several provisions whose purpose is to guarantee the caisse's independence of action. Its president is appointed for ten years, and his salary cannot be reduced. In addition, the minister of finance cannot issue guidelines to the caisse, and the caisse may act entirely as it wishes, without governmental intervention, within the limits of the powers conferred by its act of incorporation. This formal separation does not seem to have been taken seriously, and the caisse was suspected of having been involved, along with the Quebec government, in a kind of "rampant socialism."[312]

With respect to the Alberta Heritage Savings Trust Fund, there are direct organic links between the Alberta government and the fund. The provincial treasurer is responsible for managing the money, and the provincial cabinet is its investment committee. Since 1982, the fund has acquired voting shares in commercial companies (through the Commercial Investment Division) but without ever exceeding the ceiling of 5 percent of the shares issued and outstanding.[313] The decision-making mechanism used to manage the fund coincides with the views of the Alberta government, which sees itself as activist and interventionist for "the benefit of the province." This approach is controversial, since it involves the use of the fund's resources for the benefit of the province;in addition, it is feared that the very size of the fund will create distortions on the financial market, since the fund has a major advantage in comparison with private financial institutions, namely fiscal immunity, as provided by s.125 of the *Constitution Act, 1867*.[314]

## The Free Movement of Capital

Does the duality of legislative regimes for supervising financial institutions create distortions that interfere with the movement of capital within the Canadian economy as a whole? Debates over repeated attempts to extend banking legislation to all deposit institutions do not lead to such a conclusion. The argument related to the management of the monetary function has never really been accepted. Indeed, the effectiveness of the Bank of Canada's monetary policy has really not suffered from the fact that Parliament does not exercise direct and full jurisdiction over all of the institutions in question. However, a development which favours the functional regulation of financial institutions could, for reasons of equity, mean that all institutions that want to take in public deposits and to offer chequing accounts would be subject to the control of the Bank of Canada.

To justify subjecting all deposit institutions to the same authority, some observers have cited the fact that depositor confidence depends not only on the state of health of the institution with which they are dealing, but also on the security offered by other similar establishments. The creation of the Canada Deposit Insurance Corporation and the Régie d'assurance-dépôts du Québec reduced this fear by providing a safety net. By virtue of the *Investment Companies Act*, the Canada Deposit Insurance Corporation can even make short-term loans, as a lender of last resort, to consumer credit corporations controlled by Canadian residents. In order to satisfy potential short-term liquidity requirements, the corporation has also entered into agreements with the Credit Union Stabilization Corporation (Alberta), the B.C. Credit Union Reserve Board, and the Saskatchewan Credit Union Mutual Aid Board. The Economic Council of Canada, while pointing out the imperfections of the system, nevertheless concludes that it is effective.[315]

The serious crises that have affected *caisses d'entraide économique* in Quebec (since organized into Societés d'entraide économique) and certain provincial or federal trust or mortgage loan companies have, to date, not caused general panic that would be harmful to deposit institutions as a whole. It is clear that the existence of deposit-insurance has had a stabilizing influence in the face of these events, and that the cooperation of the various government bodies concerned has mitigated their consequences.[316] In addition, in January 1983, the Canada Deposit Insurance Corporation increased depositor protection from $20,000 to $60,000.[317] In short, the duality of the legislative regime does not seem to have created any significant or lasting distortions in the capital markets.

Potential diversification of the activities of deposit institutions does, however, pose a definite problem; we must "first of all revise completely the means of financing deposit insurance [translation]," as the Confédération des caisses populaires et d'économie Desjardins pointed out in its submission to the Royal Commission on the Economic Union and Development Prospects for Canada. Indeed, fairness would seem to demand that deposit institutions which diversify should pay premiums to the Canada Deposit Insurance Corporation or the Régie d'assurance-dépôts du Québec, the premiums varying according to the additional risks assumed.[318] Finally, it should be noted that the Canada Deposit Insurance scheme produced some harmonization of the rights of member institutions.[319] The recent creation of the Canadian Payments Association has allowed provincial deposit institutions full participation in the Canadian payments system. On the other hand, these institutions must first show that they are covered by a federal deposit insurance and inspection plan or by a similar provincial plan, and they must maintain a deposit account at the Bank of Canada and a margin of credit for compensation.[320]

Financial institutions have now reached a new stage as a result of automation and the development of one-stop service centres which allow clients to use one financial institution for most of their needs. This development paves the way for the advent of financial "supermarkets," and its apparent disorder is the result of the multitude of standards created not only by the application of the "four pillars" theory but also by the multiplicity of legislation involved. In any case, the circulation of capital does not seem to have suffered unduly, but, on a regulatory level, the situation creates competition whose economic effects are difficult to assess.

Finally, it is unlikely that technological progress will interfere with the free movement of capital; Parliament's legislative jurisdiction seems to us to be sufficiently all-encompassing to allow it to intervene as necessary. With respect to securities transactions, interprovincial cooperation has produced considerable harmonization, without, however, managing to avoid a certain number of irritants. Finally, the presence of institutional investors, private and public, on the financial markets causes controversy over the degree of concentration allowed, over the effectiveness of financial markets, over relations between the private sector and the public sector, and over the objectives of "building the province" or "building the country."

**Chapter 3**

# Beyond Intervention

The debate over economic mobility is basically centred on measures taken by public authorities to regulate the flow of labour, goods, services, and capital; consequently, only non-tariff barriers erected by public authorities are considered, and little attention is paid to the behaviour of other economic parties. Theoretically, the reduction or even the removal of public barriers to the free movement of goods and factors of production actually creates a free market, which can then distribute resources in the most efficient manner. But it would be foolish to neglect the influence of private-interest groups, which can also thwart this objective.

## The Power of the Private Sector

The "political" power of private companies is indisputable; it even tends to increase with the combined influence of the international division of labour, the internationalization of capital markets, and the technological revolution. In his study on the power of corporations, Professor Beck points out that the business community is, in many ways, performing a public activity when it makes its many decisions, and this fashions economic development.[321] Close business relations between various groups, strong concentration in the ownership and control of the activities of Canadian businesses, the weakness of Canadian measures to stimulate competition, interrelationships in boards of directors, close links between financial capital and industrial capital, and the participation of commercial companies in the development and formulation of government policy have all been meticulously documented and have engendered bitter debates. The business "culture" has already shown that it is capable of creating real obstructions to the movement of capital, obstructions which the market seems incapable of overcoming.[322]

## The French-speaking and English-speaking Business Communities: A Union of Solitudes?

In the 1960s, the Royal Commission on Bilingualism and Biculturalism pointed out the problems posed by the economic integration of the English-speaking and French-speaking business communities.[323] At the same time, the Comité québécois d'étude sur les institutions financières, while adhering to the principle of maximum freedom for the movement of private capital, said that this principle was meaningful only in a world in which all factors of production were perfectly mobile, including labour. But Quebec's particular cultural and linguistic character means that this mobility is only relative.[324]

Professor André Ryba's work (at the beginning of the 1970s) shows that the relative erosion of the Quebec financial sector is due to the concentration of the finance industry in Toronto.[325] In view of the importance of financial infrastructure to economic development, the Quebec government's efforts were at that time directed toward maintaining and developing the financial institutions which were likely to ensure the vitality of financial intermediaries on the provincial scene. The current reform of the Quebec scheme for regulating financial institutions is aimed at reinforcing this sector. Among other things, the modernization of securities legislation, together with a vigorous revival strategy, has in the past few years strengthened the position of the Montreal Stock Exchange. The Quebec government hopes to achieve similarly satisfactory results in the growth of other Quebec financial institutions by means of major amendments made recently to its insurance legislation and through amendments to be made in the near future to the legislative framework governing trust companies and caisses populaires.[326]

The French-speaking financial sector has developed apart from the English-speaking business world[327] and the coexistence of the two is still marked by a certain chauvinism, as the Laurentian Group pointed out in its submission to this Commission:

> The "entrepreneurship" of Quebeckers is also threatened, on the one hand by the fact that certain provinces and a portion of their business communities are not very receptive and, on the other hand, within Quebec, by a chauvinism toward anything which is foreign to us [translation].[328]

From this point of view, it is interesting to note that a significant number of members of the press and of the French-speaking business world in Quebec have perceived the federal Bill S-31 as a means of preventing French-dominated financial agencies from counteracting the English-speaking hold over major economic organizations.[329]

To correct the relative weakness of the French-speaking business community, Quebec has taken a liberal attitude toward local and foreign private investment, and it has tried to educate the powerful public sector in order to attain the priority objectives which the market has denied it.[330] It is in this context that the Caisse de dépôt et placement du Québec was created in 1965, and was given the mandate of stimulating growth in Quebec and of administering its funds with care. One of the supplementary objectives which the founders of the Caisse de dépôt et placement du Québec had in mind was to expand the bond market in Quebec in order to free the government from the monopoly of certain financial agents.[331]

The strategic importance of the caisse was confirmed in the report of the Comité d'étude sur les institutions financières (1969), which recommended channelling money from Quebec public-sector pension funds to the caisse to enable it to become "as large as possible" as soon as possible. A decade later, the Groupe de travail sur l'épargne au Québec, while insisting on the predominant role of the trust bond (defined as a bond which gives the best financial return compatible with security of capital and the nature of the liabilities), showed a keen interest in the participation of the caisse in the economic development of Quebec.[332]

According to a recent survey, Quebec business leaders' perception of the caisse is that there is a gulf between French-speaking people, who support it, and English-speaking people, who remain guarded. On the other hand, a majority in each group fears that there will be "cautious nationalization [translation]," both directly and through the caisse's association with other organizations, private or public, in order to control companies.[333] The caisse has become the obvious symbol of the French-speaking presence among major financial institutions in Canada, and it is perceived by many as a bridgehead of "French power" in financial circles. It sometimes acts as a regular merchant bank by facilitating the reorganization of companies or the creation of conglomerates, and it has certainly had a significant impact on the industrial structure of Quebec.[334] The debate on reassessing the mandate and the structure of the caisse continues. Thus, the Conseil du patronat du Québec has advocated dividing the caisse into several autonomous entities, each in competition with the others, and of reducing from 30 to 10 percent the number of voting shares which it may own in a company.[335]

## Tension Between Central and Western Canada

The western provinces have always been suspicious of Canadian banks, accusing them of stimulating central Canadian development at their expense. This frustration has provoked numerous attempts on their part to establish financial institutions that are capable of meeting their needs.[336] In 1973, the Conference on Economic Prospects for the West provided the setting for a confrontation on this point between the governments of the western provinces, the federal government, and the major banks, a confrontation which centred on the federal government's proposal to allow one or more of the provinces to own jointly up to 25 percent of the participating capital of a new bank, and then to reduce this proportion to 10 percent within an agreed period of time.[337] This idea was gradually accepted, and in spite of the opposition of the Senate standing committee on banking, trade, and commerce, it was finally incorporated into the *Bank Act* in 1980.[338] Moreover, in the spring of 1984, through the Alberta Heritage Savings Trust Fund, the Alberta government took the opportunity which presented itself to acquire 5 percent of the share capital of the recently established Bank of Alberta.

In addition, in its 1984 white paper on industrial and science policies for Alberta, the Alberta government repeated its historical claims and announced its intentions with respect to the growth of regional financial institutions. Summarizing the events of the last decade (the creation of regional banks, the installation of senior officials of major Canadian banks in Alberta, and the particular role which has devolved to treasury branches), the white paper concludes: "With head offices here, entrepreneurs can feel they are relating to senior decision-makers who share similar backgrounds and information."[339] The policy statement listed and suggested several scenarios for managing local deposit institutions and for revitalizing the Alberta Stock Exchange, and it calculated the potential advantages of the development of an "Alberta" insurance industry. ("An Alberta-based life insurance industry would be more aware of and sensitive to a wide range of investment opportunities here.")[340]

The promotion of western financial interests took a spectacular step forward with the inauguration of the Alberta Heritage Savings Trust Fund in 1976. The premier of Alberta, Peter Lougheed, said at that time that the fund had four primary objectives, namely:

- to create a source of income to take over from the development of non-renewable resources in Alberta when they are depleted;
- to reduce the necessity of public borrowing;
- to improve the quality of life; and
- to diversify and consolidate the Alberta economy.[341]

The fund has been used to advantage to protect Albertans from the "rainy days" of the recession, and it will be called upon to play an important role in the plan for industrial and technological revival, which was announced by the Alberta government in the summer of 1984.[342] With $13.7 billion in resources (at March 31, 1984) and predictions of rapid growth (despite a temporary reduction from 30 percent to 15 percent in the transfer of income from natural non-renewable resources and in the payment of its net income into the province's consolidated fund),[343] the fund is viewed with some suspicion in various financial and political circles.

Another example of the political willingness of western provincial governments to participate directly in the financial sector is the enactment by the British Columbia legislature, in 1975, of the *Savings and Trust Corporation of British Columbia Act*.[344] Although it has not yet been promulgated, this act nevertheless reflects the willingness of British Columbia to compete with market forces when necessary.

## Conclusion

In summary, intervention by provincial public authorities in capital markets meets their desire to deal with certain regional irritants or imbalances. If it is not accompanied by carefully considered exceptions, the incorporation into the Constitution of the principle of the free movement of capital could seriously interfere with desirable interventions in the capital markets, without, however, reducing antagonism between interest groups. Thus, the creation of powerful public financial intermediaries whose legitimacy is derived from the legislatures which control them, such as the Caisse de dépôt et placement du Québec and the Alberta Heritage Savings Trust Fund, balances two distinct political concepts. Building the province and building Canada, it challenges the traditional concept of the respective roles of the federal government and the provincial governments in building a Canadian common market and in developing the economy in general. On another level, it represents the whole issue of direct government investment in the private sector, to which there is strong opposition.[345]

# Chapter 4

# Proposals for Reform:
## *A Historical Review*

Some of the private and public groups that were involved in the issue of the free movement of capital during the 1970s have proposed various amendments to the Constitution. The Canadian Bar Association has suggested that there should be included in the Constitution the principle that Canada constitutes an economic union, and a provision (clearly inspired by the terminology of European Economic Community law) which provides for "the acceptance of goods, services and *capital* from one province by each of the other provinces without imposing duties or quotas, fees or other similar measures, except if necessary for reasons of health or public safety [translation]." The bar association felt that the "health" and "public safety" exceptions were sufficient for the courts to confirm the validity of measures for protecting the public, such as those dealing with guaranteed deposits in the field of insurance.[346]

The Task Force on Canadian Unity affirmed that "the Constitution should make clear the prohibition of barriers to the interprovincial movement of capital."[347] At the same time, in Ontario, the advisory committee on Confederation expressed its approval of the formal incorporation, in the Constitution, of the principle of mobility for individuals, capital, goods, and information, but it hastened to add that provincial statutes which have secondary or minor effects on the mobility of the above should not be quashed. On the other hand, Ontario's special legislative committee on constitutional reform is opposed to the constitutionalization of the concept of a common market, preferring to leave to the mechanisms of intergovernmental relations the resolution of potential disputes. The then Premier of Ontario, William G. Davis, had, however, previously expressed his hope that the Canadian Constitution would formally recognize the principle of the free movement of capital.[348] In its white paper entitled *La nouvelle entente Québec-Canada*, the Government of Quebec, while embracing the principle of the free movement of capital, concluded laconically that "each party could promulgate an investment code or, if necessary, adopt special rules applicable to certain financial institutions [translation]."[349]

In its 1980 beige paper on the renewal of the Canadian federation, the Quebec Liberal party expressed its support for the formal inclusion in the Canadian Constitution of the principle of the free movement of capital within the Canadian economy, subject to the power of the provinces to enact non-discriminatory laws of general application, to regulate the investment of certain financial institutions, and to enact laws with respect to health, public safety, and professional organization. However, while embracing the principle of the free movement of factors of production within the Canadian economic union, the Quebec Liberal party has since abandoned a constitutional solution (an improved s.121), indicating that it would prefer to see an interprovincial code of ethics implemented. The major advantage of such a code would be that it would avoid the strictness and rigidity of the judicial process while maintaining the flexibility of the political process for resolving conflicts.[350]

The Canadian government explained the theoretical bases for its demand for increased economic power at the time of the meeting of the continuing committee of ministers on the Constitution (July 1980).[351] Challenging restrictions on the free movement of capital within the Canadian economic union, it affirmed that "there are compelling reasons for securing in the Constitution the basic of national rules of our economic union and for ensuring that both orders of government abide by these rules" while at the same time admitting, on the other hand that "the constitutional securing of absolute economic mobility within Canada would obviously be incompatible with the maintenance of a federal system." And it concluded that, "wherever they may have been born or have chosen to reside in the country, Canadians should be free to take up residence, to acquire and hold property, to gain a livelihood . . . in any province or territory of Canada, provided that they abide by the laws of general application of that province or territory [translation]."[352] However, its specific suggestion with respect to capital took the form of expanding the scope of s.121 and s.91(2) of the *Constitution Act, 1867* rather than adding to the proposed s.6 of the *Canadian Charter of Rights and Freedoms*, which achieved this objective only "in part."[353] The proposed s.121 and s.91(2) read as follows:

121(1) Neither Canada nor a province shall by law or practice discriminate in a manner that unduly impedes the operation of the Canadian economic union, directly or indirectly, on the basis of the province or territory of residence or former residence of a person, on the basis of the province or territory of origin or destination of goods, services or capital, or on the basis of the province or territory into which or from which goods, services or capital are imported or exported.

(2) Nothing in subsection (1) renders invalid a law of Parliament or of a legislature enacted in the interests of public safety, order, health or morale.

(3) Nothing in subsection (1) renders invalid a law of Parliament enacted pursuant to the principles of equalization and regional development to which Parliament and the legislatures are committed or declared by Parliament to be in an overriding national interest or enacted pursuant to an international obligation undertaken by Canada.

(4) Nothing in subsection (2) or (3) renders valid a law of Parliament or a legislature that impedes the admission free into any province of goods, services or capital originating in or imported into any other province or territory.

91(2) The regulation of trade and commerce in goods, services and capital.

(2)(1) The regulation of competition throughout Canada and the establishment of product standards applicable throughout Canada where such regulation or such standards are reasonably necessary for the operation of the Canadian economic union.[354]

The present s.121 establishes the notion of a pan-Canadian common market with respect to the movement of goods, and some people believe that its prescriptions can be enforced against both Parliament and the provincial legislatures. This section does not confer specific legislative jurisdiction on either of the two levels of government; it is, rather, intended as a brake to the obstacles or impediments to the interprovincial movement of goods. The courts have not, however, given it sufficient scope to establish it as a truly constitutional method of protecting economic integration.

The drafters intended that the "improved" s.121 would proscribe legal or usual barriers to economic mobility, but without undue restrictions on government measures with legitimate objectives. The expression "in a manner that unduly impedes" (in paragraph 1) would probably have had no significance, since the court would have assumed that a law or administrative measure ratified by a public authority is, by its very nature, in the public interest and does not therefore unduly impede. The exceptions listed in paragraphs 2 and 3 are similar to the usual list of police powers. It should be pointed out that such exceptions could only be imposed by an act and not by administrative measures. Paragraph 4 upholds the prohibition contemplated in the existing s.121 with respect to interprovincial customs barriers on goods, and has extended it to services and to capital.

It is interesting to note that paragraph 3 says, for the benefit of the central government only, that its legislation can derogate from the principle of the free movement of capital to respect the requirements of regional development, equalization, the national interest, or international agreements. In fact, the wording of paragraph 3 implies that Parliament is empowered to amend legislation passed by the legislatures for purposes of applying international treaties. The exception for the "national interest" means that, for all practical purposes, Parliament's power to legislate to limit economic mobility would no longer be subject to the constraints of the first paragraph of the proposed s.121. Indeed, it seems unlikely that the courts would question the validity of a declaration of national interest by Parliament. In short, according to the text that was proposed initially by the federal government, the provinces would have had to have accepted much stronger restrictions, since Parliament alone was empowered to use proscribed methods to satisfy the perceived need for intervention.

Saskatchewan replied by tabling its own bill, which was designed to incorporate into the Constitution a simple declaration of principle, which stated that the Canadian economic union should be maintained and developed, and a non-imperative agreement between Parliament and the legislatures to respect, in their actions, the free movement of people, goods, services, and capital, as well as the uniformity of laws, policies, and federal and provincial practices governing the Canadian economic union.[355]

The preparatory work of the continuing committee of ministers on the Constitution gave birth to four draft bills which were brought to the attention of the premiers at the time of the federal-provincial conference on the Constitution, in September 1980. Draft Bill 1 was basically the same as the original federal government bill, but as far as capital is concerned, it considerably enlarged the exceptions offered to the provinces by adding measures of "public interest" and the reduction of economic inequalities between the regions of a province. The expression "in a manner that unduly impedes" was replaced by "in an unduly harmful manner." In addition, the process of enforcement provided for in paragraph 7 denoted a clear desire for "dejudicialization," since it was provided therein that a law or a practice deemed unacceptable was nevertheless valid, unless it was abrogated by the appropriate authority or was not ratified by the second chamber (which was then contemplated). The second draft bill substituted "non-discrimination" for "in a manner that unduly impedes."

Ontario's suggestion (Draft Bill 3), which favoured the expansion of the scope of s.121 to guarantee the free movement of citizens, goods, services, and capital, was basically a repetition of the first two draft bills, but it eliminated the concept of a restrictive list of exceptions, including the national interest, in favour of a general test (Parliament and the legislatures would be prevented from establishing usage contrary to the principle of mobility and from passing an act which in essence and in substance was incompatible with it). Saskatchewan again suggested simply passing a declaration affirming the existence of an economic union and the non-restrictive adherence of Parliament and the legislatures to the principle of the free movement of capital.[356] Finally, the inclusion of the term "capital" in s.91(2) amended Parliament's legislative power only and, in the absence of a similar amendment by the provincial authorities, was likely to produce a considerable increase in Parliament's legislative powers in areas, such as the regulation of securities and that of provincially incorporated financial institutions, which are currently under provincial jurisdiction.[357]

The provinces all reacted differently to the inclusion in the Constitution of enforceable standards guaranteeing freedom of movement for factors of production, especially capital. Manitoba and Quebec were strictly opposed to it; British Columbia and New Brunswick expressed their reservations; Saskatchewan, Alberta, and Newfoundland also agreed to incorporating a declaration of principle into the Constitution; Nova Scotia and Ontario were generally in agreement with the federal government.[358]

Saskatchewan's substantial argument touched on all aspects of the issue. That province recalled that "a very large proportion of these obstacles are created voluntarily by the two levels of government in order to achieve other social and economic objectives to which the political authorities attach the greatest priority. They simply constitute the initiatives of a responsible government, which is the very essence of our democratic regime [translation]." In addition, in concentrating its attention only on the explicit obstacles to economic mobility, the federal proposal ignored other far more important practices, such as personal and corporate income tax, and national policies with respect to transport duties and tariffs. Finally, for Saskatchewan, the recourse to courts of law for resolving basically social or economic conflicts seemed most inappropriate, since it opened the door to legal disputes over lending policies of the Saskatchewan Heritage Fund and over government financial support for provincial enterprises. Extending the scope of the existing s.121 to capital thus ran the risk of fostering judicial interpretation that would prohibit any important direct or indirect interference.[359]

In the fever of the constitutional negotiations of 1980–81, the case for strengthening the Canadian common market was abandoned in favour of inserting into the Constitution the *Canadian Charter of Rights and Freedoms*. Once this step had been accomplished, it did not take long for a liberal interpretation of the Charter to be demanded in order to guarantee the free movement of capital in the context of the promotion of individual economic rights. Future suggestions for constitutional reform could, therefore, quite easily spark lively debate on the advisability of including in the Charter, rather than in s.121 of the Constitution, the principle of the free movement of factors of production. In its provisional report entitled *Challenges and Choices*, the Royal Commission on the Economic Union and Development Prospects for Canada has demonstrated clear concern over this matter.[360]

## Various Solutions

As mechanisms for reinforcing the Canadian economic union, the possibility of either an improved version of s.121 of the *Constitution Act, 1867* or an expansion of s.6 of the *Canadian Charter of Rights and Freedoms*, or even the enactment of an interprovincial code of ethics, would all formally inscribe the principle of the free movement of capital into the institutional fabric of the country; but, depending upon the solution adopted, it would also reflect very different interpretations of this principle.

An addition to s.6 of the Charter would probably confirm adherence to the laissez-faire principle, in which the primacy of individual rights is legitimately opposed to the efforts of the public authorities to regulate the economy. American experience prior to Roosevelt's New Deal provides an eloquent example of a reduction in the power of public authorities in the face of liberal imperatives evoked in substantive due process. The Supreme Court of the United States had to undergo a veritable judicial revolution (as distinct from the process of amending the Constitution, which is within the political arena) in order to break the impasse and authorize vigorous government intervention in economic matters.[361] In Australia, the adherence of the Privy Council and the Australian High Court to the primacy, in the commerce clause, of individual economic rights over the two levels of government created strong jurisprudential tensions and created legal confusion and insecurity. In the extreme, this approach prevents the public authorities from monopolizing an economic activity in the public interest, because the validity of such a decision is evaluated not in terms of the public interest but in terms of the harm caused to individuals (microeconomic approach).[362] In the Canadian constitutional context, the exception in s.1 of the Charter could undoubtedly be invoked to defend government decisions. However, the Supreme Court's view of the scope of this section remains unknown. As for the exercise of the right of override provided for in s.33, this would offer (if it survives) an escape which makes the insertion of the principle itself illusory. Finally, it would be very interesting to specify prior to any reform of this nature, whether legal entities, as well as individuals, would be able to benefit from this constitutional protection.

A likely consequence of the extension of s.121 would be that this section would assume the role of protecting economic integration in a negative way, a function that is presently performed in an equivocal fashion by s.91(2). To the extent that the federal government's legislative and executive authority is subject to s.121, and where the exceptions are actually restricted, this provision would impose the same constraints on the legislative and administrative powers of the federal or provincial authorities. In addition, s.121, extended to capital, could include harmonization by means of judicial interpretation of the exceptions provided by the act. Thus, we have mentioned the contradictory decisions of the Quebec and Ontario securities commissions with respect to ownership and the diversification of stockbrokers. One of them (Quebec) has taken a liberal attitude to both ownership and diversification, on the grounds that the public interest and security are not threatened, whereas the other (Ontario) has suggested the creation of barriers to both ownership and diversification, on the grounds of its own perception of the public interest. What will become of the Ontario position in the case of a judicial dispute in which it is necessary to prove the need for public protection?

One of the most difficult problems presented by the possibility of reformulating s.121 is related to the economic vision which it is supposed to reflect. Australia deserves special attention in this regard, since the commerce clause in its constitution already contains the principle of free trade within the Australian common market. Although torn between the tenets of individual economic rights and individuals who prefer a free-trade approach, and taking into consideration a pragmatic balance of the overall interests involved, the Privy Council and the Australian High Court have, over the years, maintained an approach based on individual economic rights, characterized by confusion, rigidity, frequent doctrinal changes of direction, profound reticence, and the fact that it is impossible for the court to take major economic debates into account. In the context of the Canadian Constitution, it seems likely that the courts would reject an individualist interpretation of an amended s.121, assuming that if this had been the intention of the drafters, the principle would have been incorporated into the Charter (clearly, nothing is less certain). According to this hypothesis, the problem of the interpretation of s.121 does not disappear as such but becomes an examination of the nature and scope of a free-trade approach (mainly concerned with macroeconomics).

Thus, it could be claimed that only discriminatory protectionist measures are hit with sanctions, namely those that treat foreign investors differently (and detrimentally) from others in the same jurisdiction; in this regard, s.6 of the Charter, dealing with mobility rights, uses provincial boundaries as a test, which is surprising in the context of fundamental individual rights. Another problem related to the discriminatory approach is whether we must limit ourselves to a formal analysis of legislation or whether we may also closely examine the practical discriminatory effects of legislation that is formally non-discriminatory. In the context of the fight against protectionism by eliminating discrimination, the courts would have to invalidate any law or administrative practice allowed by a province or by the central government which conferred a significant economic advantage (formally or in practice, depending upon the type of approach) on one province at the expense of another. On the other hand, failure to confirm the existence of such a phenomenon would render the disputed law or administrative practice valid. The proposals put forward by the federal government and the Ontario government in 1980–81 (both of which favoured expanding the scope of s.121 to cover capital) were based on the criteria of discrimination.

The reformulation of s.6 of the *Canadian Charter of Rights and Free-*

*doms* or of s.121 of the *Constitution Act, 1867* would entail an increase in the prerogatives of judicial power to the detriment of parliamentary sovereignty. The American and Australian examples show to what extent the results obtained reflect the structure of the process itself (separate analysis of each individual case, constraint of stare decisis, rigidity and confusion in results). In the United States, the Supreme Court has literally (and unilaterally) removed its yoke by recognizing the supremacy of congressional decisions with respect to interstate commerce, whereas in Australia the process of adjudication according to the commerce clause remains unclear.

An interprovincial code of ethics, formulated by a joint federal-provincial commission, would at least have the benefit of flexibility in its creation and subsequent adaptation. Such a commission could provide a forum for various formulae and could attempt to achieve a delicate balance between respect for parliamentary sovereignty over economic matters and the requirements of the harmonious operation of the Canadian common market. What is more, the right to bring an action against a regulatory agency could be left to provincial attorney generals which would reinforce the intergovernmental character of the mechanism adopted.

## Conclusion

By means of its structural division of legislative powers, the Canadian Constitution implicitly recognizes the limits of the exercise of any right (except with respect to the prohibitions set forth by the *Canadian Charter of Rights and Freedoms*). In this context, the role of the courts is limited to identifying who, the central authority or the member states, is empowered to regulate an activity. An unavoidable consequence of this system is that the federal and provincial legislatures are theoretically in a position to control, if not block, the flow of capital within the Canadian economic union according to their own objectives.

The Constitution of Canada, unlike that of Australia, does not contain any method of negative protection of the free movement of capital which can be used against the two levels of government, except with respect to guarantees of personal mobility provided in s.6 of the *Canadian Charter of Rights and Freedoms*. However, this provision's wording, the history of its formulation and incorporation into the Charter, and the Supreme Court's first comments on the subject, lead us to believe that, as we have already mentioned, it is not appropriate to interpret the provision liberally to the point of actually creating a means of promoting and protecting the free movement of capital in order to provide free access to all sectors of economic activity. With regard to extending the scope of s.121 to include capital, such an amendment would probably allow the debate to continue at a global level where the general interests of the various public authorities would be taken into account. However, the "judicialization" of the process of resolving these differences does not appear to be the best way to achieve the objectives of flexibility and speed, nor does it facilitate what should essentially be a political arbitration. A code of ethics applied by a joint national commission would therefore seem to be a more attractive practical solution, and it would likely be accepted voluntarily and positively by the federal and provincial authorities. Finally, such an approach recognizes the limited nature of consensus and the theoretical bases necessary to justify a more limited and more rigid intervention in the form of an amendment to the Constitution.

## Notes

1. The concept of the "movement of capital" needs to be clarified in order to minimize overlap with the concepts of "the free movement of goods or the free circulation of services":

   "The free movement of capital is distinct from transfers connected with the goods, services, or the movement of manpower, and includes the unrestricted right of nationals of member States to acquire, transfer and utilize within the boundaries of the Community, capital originating within the Community" (Étienne Sadi Kirschen et al., *Financial Integration in Western Europe*, New York: Columbia University Press, 1969, p. 41).

2. Ivan Bernier, "Le concept d'union économique dans la Constitution canadienne: de l'intégration commerciale à l'intégration des facteurs de production" (1979), 20 *Cahiers de droit* 177, 179–80; Jean Chrétien, *Securing the Canadian Economic Union in the Constitution* (Ottawa: Minister of Supply and Services Canada, 1980), pp. 1–6; James Leavy, *La clause de commerce et l'intégration économique* (Montreal: Éditions Thémis, 1982), p. 54; Canadian Bar Association, *Towards a New Canada* (Ottawa: Canadian Bar Foundation, 1978), p. 96. See also Jean-Charles Bonenfant, "Les origines économiques et les dispositions financières de l' Acte de l'Amérique du Nord Britannique," in B. Comeau (ed.), *Économie québécoise* (Montreal: Presses de l'Université du Québec, 1969), p. 89; Gil Rémillard, "Les intentions des Pères de la Confédération" (1979), 20 *Cahiers de droit* 797; A. Cairns, "The Judicial Committee and its Critics" (1971), 4 *Canadian Journal of Political Science* 301; A.E. Safarian, *Canadian Federalism and Economic Integration* (Ottawa: Information Canada, 1974, pp. 1–3.

3. Ivan Bernier, Nicolas Roy, Charles Pentland and Daniel Soberman, "The Concept of Economic Union in International and Constitutional Law," in *Perspectives on the Canadian Economic Union*, volume 60 of the research studies prepared for the Royal Commission on the Economic Union and Development Prospects for Canada (Toronto: University of Toronto Press, 1985).

4. See Bela Balassa, *The Theory of Economic Integration* (Homewood, Ill.): R.D. Irwin, 1961), p. 92. See also John Whalley, "Induced Distortions of Interprovincial Activity: An Overview of Issues," in M.J. Trebilcock, J.R.S. Prichard, T.J. Courchene and J. Whalley, *Federalism and the Canadian Union* (Toronto: University of Toronto Press for the Ontario Economic Council, 1983), pp. 161 et seq.; Canada, Ministry of Finance, *White Paper on the Review of Canadian Banking Legislation* (Ottawa: Minister of Supply and Services, 1976), p. 8.

5. Conseil du patronat du Québec, Submission to the Royal Commission on the Economic Union and Development Prospects for Canada, paper no. 467, p. 11; Bank of Montreal, "The Canadian Economy in Transition," brief no. 933 to the Macdonald Commission, p. 36; Quebec Liberal Party, Submission to the Royal Commission on the Economic Union and Development Prospects for Canada, presented by Robert Bourassa, submission no. 1145, February 1984, pp. 19 and 20 (favours the adoption of a code of ethics); Richard Hatfield, *Transcripts* of the Royal Commission

on the Economic Union and Development Prospects for Canada, volume 15, Fredericton, September 23, 1983, pp. 3595–97.

6. Whalley, *supra*, n. 4, p. 162.

7. *Idem*, pp. 163, 165 and 166.

8. J. Robert Prichard and Jamie Benidickson, *Securing the Canadian Economic Union: Federalism and Internal Barriers to Trade* in M.J. Trebilcock, J.R.S. Prichard, T.J. Courchene and J. Whalley, *Federalism and the Canadian Union*, Toronto, University of Toronto Press for the Ontario Economic Council, 1983, p. 8 and 9. The Economic Council of Canada, in its paper on financial intervention by the government in support of the private sector, summarizes the rationality of government policies as follows:

> There are four major elements of market failure that may warrant government intervention in financial markets: obstacles to the proper internal functioning of the financial markets themselves, externalities, public goods and uninsurable risks. The existence of any one of these can hinder the efficient allocation of financial resources and may thus prevent society from achieving desired economic and social equilibrium. To these 'internal' motives for intervention may be added a fifth: problems arising in other markets which might best be resolved through measures taken in financial markets, (Economic Council of Canada; *Intervention and Efficiency: A Study of Government Credit and Credit Guarantees to the Private Sector* (Ottawa: Minister of Supply and Services Canada, 1982), p. 11).

9. Canadian Bar Association, *supra*, note 2, p. 99. See also Bernier, *supra*, n. 2, p. 219.

10. Bernier et al., *supra*, note 3. See also G.V. La Forest, *The Allocation of Taxing Power Under the Canadian Constitution*, 2nd ed. (Toronto: Canadian Tax Foundation, 1981), pp. 178–82.

11. See Emilio Binavince, "The Impact of the Mobility Rights: The Canadian Economic Union — A Boom or a Bust?" (1982), 14 *Ottawa Law Review* 340, at pp. 355 and 356; Douglas A. Schmeiser and Katherine J. Young, "Mobility Rights in Canada" in Canadian Institute for the Administration of Justice, *La Charte canadienne des droits et libertés — ses débats, ses problèmes, son avenir* (Montreal: Les Éditions Yvon Blais, 1983), pp. 197–203. With regard to the constitutional debates of 1980–81 on the movement of capital, see chap. 4, "Proposals for Reform," in this paper.

12. With respect to applying s.6 of the *Canadian Charter of Rights and Freedoms* to companies, see Pierre Blache, "The Mobility Rights (Section 6)," in W.S. Tarnopolsky and G.A. Beaudoin (eds.), *Canadian Charter of Rights and Freedoms* (Montreal: Wilson and Lafleur, 1982), pp. 239–55; Morris Manning, *Rights, Freedoms and the Courts: A Practical Analysis of the Constitution Act, 1982.* (Toronto: Emond-Montgomery, 1983), pp. 223 and 224; Davies, Ward and Beck, Barristers and Solicitors, *The Impact of the Canadian Charter of Rights and Freedoms on Canadian Business Law* (Toronto, January 1983), pp. 26 and 27; Schmeiser and Young, *supra*, n. 11, pp. 197 and 198; William Moull, "Business Law Implications of the Canadian Charter of Rights and Freedoms" (1923–84), 8 *Can. Bus. L.J.* 448 at pp. 472–75.

As for expanding the application of the *Canadian Charter of Rights and Freedoms* to transactions between private parties, the prevailing opinion is that such a conclusion, although tempting, goes against the current of the constitutional debates that preceded the enacting of the Charter and contradicts its general structure (see W.S. Tarnopolsky, "The Equality Rights in the Canadian Charter of Rights and Freedoms" (1983), 61 *Can. Bar Rev.* 242, at p. 255 et seq., Katherine Swinton, "Application of the Canadian Charter of Rights and Freedoms" in W.S. Tarnopolsky and G.A. Beaudoin (eds.), *Canadian Charter of Rights and Freedoms* (Montreal: Wilson and Lafleur, 1982), pp. 44–49. For a contrary opinion, see Dale Gibson, "The Charter of Rights and the Private Sector" (1982–83), 12 *Man. L.J.* 214; Dale Gibson, "Distinguishing the Governors from the Governed: The Meaning of 'Government' Under Section 32(1) of the Charter, in Canadian Institute for the Administration of Justice, *La Charte canadienne des droits et libertés — ses débats, ses problèmes, son avenir* (Montreal: Les Éditions Yvon Blais, 1983), pp. 71–76; Moull, *supra*, note 12, p. 456 et seq. Moreover, the Supreme Court has opted for an interpretation of s. 6 which respects the general context of its incorporation in the Charter (see *Skapinker v. Law Society of Upper Canada* (1983), 53 N.R. 169 (S.C.C.)).

13. *The Queen v. Fishermen's Wharf Limited* (1982), 135 D.L.R. (3d) 307. This decision has been quite rightly criticized by G.J. Brandt (see G.J. Brandt, "Canadian Charter of Rights and Freedoms — Right to Property as an Extension of Personal Security — Status of Undeclared Rights" (1983), 61 *Can. Bar Rev.* 398). In addition, Mr. Justice La Forest of the New Brunswick Court of Appeal implicitly dismissed the comments of Mr. Justice Dixon at first instance [*Queen in right of New Brunswick v. Estabrooks Pontiac Buick Ltd., The Queen in right of New Brunswick v. Fishermen's Wharf Ltd.* (1982), 144 D.L.R. (3d) 21]. See also John D. Whyte, "Fundamental Justice: The Scope and Application of Section 7 of the Charter," in Canadian Institute for the Administration of Justice, *La Charte canadienne des droits et libertés — ses débats, ses problèmes, son avenir* (Montreal: Les Éditions Yvan Blais, 1983), pp. 38–41; *Re Workers' Compensation Board of Nova Scotia and Coastal Rentals, Sales and Service Ltd.* (November 3, 1983, Nova Scotia Supreme Court), *Canadian Charter of Rights Annotated*, pp. 12–19.

For the historical aspects of the debate about enshrining the right to property in the Constitution, see Edward McWhinney, *Canada and the Constitution 1979–82: Patriation and the Charter of Rights* (Toronto: University of Toronto Press, 1982), pp. 88, 112; Roy Romanow, John Whyte, and Howard Leeson, *Canada Notwithstanding — The Making of the Constitution 1976–82* (Toronto: Carswell/Methuen, 1984), pp. 231, 232, 237, and 243.

In addition to resolving the problem of expanding the guarantees provided in s. 7 of the Charter, the courts will undoubtedly soon have to decide whether such guarantees are simply procedural or whether, on the contrary, the courts may examine the very substance of legislative provisions or disputed executive measures. (see Whyte, *supra*, note 13, pp. 21–41); Luc Tremblay, "Section 7 of the Charter: Substantive Due Process?" (1984), 2 *U.B.C. L. Rev.* 201.

14. Section 15 of the Charter should be read in conjunction with Section 28, which provides that "notwithstanding anything in this Charter, the rights and freedoms referred to in it are guaranteed equally to male and female persons." In addition, it should be remembered that the guarantees of equality provided for in s. 15 probably include only the actions of public authorities and not those of private individuals (see Tarnopolsky, *supra*, note 12, pp. 255 et seq.). As regards the protection of the right to property, see *Canadian Bill of Rights*, S.C. 1960, c. 44, s. 1a; *Alberta Bill of Rights*, R.S.A. 1980, c. A-16, s. 1(a); *Charter of Human Rights and Freedoms*, R.S.Q. 1977, c. C-12, ss. 6 and 24; *The Saskatchewan Human Rights Code*, S.S. 1979, c. S-24-1, s. 9. See W.S. Tarnopolsky, *The Canadian Bill of Rights*, 2nd rev. ed. (Toronto: McClelland, 1975), p. 218–35; *National Capital Commission v. Lapointe*, [1972] F.C. 568, p. 570 and 571. It should be pointed out that the *Canadian Bill of Rights* as well as the provincial charters remain in force in spite of the enactment of the *Canadian Charter of Rights and Freedoms* (see s. 26 of the Charter in this regard).

15. See Task Force on Canadian Unity, *Coming to Terms* (Ottawa: Minister of Supply and Services Canada, 1979), p. 27. With regard to the history of Canadian monetary unification, see Vély Leroy, *La question monétaire en rapport avec le Québec*, (Quebec: Ministère des Affaires intergouvernementales, 1978), pp. 35–59.

16. *Constitution Act, 1867*, 30–31 Victoria, c. 3 (U.K.), s. 91 (2), (14), (15), (16), (18), (19) and (20).

17. Bernier, *supra*, n. 2, pp. 219 and 220; Peter W. Hogg, "Freedom of Movement of Goods, Persons, Services and Capital: Canadian Case Law" (1980), 3 *Revue d'intégration européenne* 301, at pp. 309 and 310, citing Bora Laskin, *Canadian Constitutional Law*, 3rd ed. (Toronto: Carswell, 1969), p. 603. This point of view is also shared by the federal government; see Chrétien, *supra*, n. 2, p. 24; and Canada, "Economic Power," document no. 830-81/006 in *Meeting of Continuing Committee of Ministers on the Constitution* (Ottawa: Canadian Intergovernmental Conference Secretariat, 1980), p. 2.

18. *Alberta Statutes Reference*, [1938] S.C.R. 100, p. 113. The *Alberta Social Credit Act* was held to be unconstitutional by five of the six members of the court on the ground

that it dealt with "banks and the incorporation of banks," and also by three of them because it dealt with currency and the regulation of trade and commerce. See also *Canadian Pioneer Management Ltd. v. Saskatchewan Labour Relations Board*, [1980] 1 S.C.R. 433, pp. 455 and 456, (hereafter *Canadian Pioneer Management Ltd.*); and Patrick N. McDonald, "The B.N.A. Act and the Nearbanks, a Case Study in Federalism" (1972), 10 *Alta. L. Rev.* 155, pp. 183 et seq.

19. Decision in *Canadian Pioneer Management Ltd.*, *supra*, n. 18, pp. 455 and 458 (Beetz).

20. *Reference re Anti-Inflation Act*, [1976] 2 S.C.R. 373, pp. 426 and 427 (Judson, Spence, Dickson and Laskin). Beetz and de Grandpré JJ felt that it was not appropriate to give Parliament unlimited jurisdiction in the field of monetary policy (idem, pp. 452 and 458). Martland, Ritchie and Pidgeon JJ expressed no opinion on this point.

21. *Constitution Act, 1867*, 30–31 Victoria, c. 3 (U.K.) s. 91(19); *Crédit foncier franco-canadien v. Ross* (1937), 3 D.L.R. 36 5 (Alta. C.A.); *Lethbridge Nor Irrigation Dist. Trustees v. I.O.F.* (1940), A.C. 513; *A.-G. Saskatchewan v. A.-G. Canada* (1949), A.C. 110; "Le gouvernement central [peut], en principe, contrôler les taux d'intérêt de toutes les institutions financières" ("The central government [may], in principle, control the interest rates of all financial institutions") (Quebec, Comité d'étude sur les institutions financières, *Rapport* (Québec: Gouvernement du Québec, 1969), p. 246, n. 1. As regards the historical aspects of government policy with respect to interest rates, see E.P. Neufeld, *The Financial System of Canada* (Toronto: Macmillan, 1972), pp. 542–71.

22. *The Constitution Act, 1867*, 30–31 Victoria, c. 3(U.K.), s. 91(15), (18), (20) and (14) (R.V.). See McDonald, *supra*, n. 18, p, 186; Bruce Welling, *Electronic Funds Transfer and the British North America Act*, Ontario Funds Transfer Study Project, document no. 6, December 1978, pp. 11 and 12.
The rapid development of electronic transfers is already seen as a phenomenon which must be taken into account in the establishment of the government's monetary policy; in fact, such transfers to a great extent facilitate the international movement of capital and the speed of monetary transactions. (See Jake V. Knoppers-Gestinfo Inc., *Report on Vulnerability Issues*, paper prepared for the Working Group on Sovereignty Aspects, Interdepartmental Task Force on Transborder Data Flows, Ottawa, December 1982, pp. 43 and 64.

23. Canadian Bar Association, *supra*, n. 2, p. 114.

24. Near-banks are "les institutions financières qui reçoivent des dépôts du public sans être titulaires d'une charte délivrée en vertu de la *Loi sur les banques*. Les quasi-banques regroupent principalement les sociétées de fiducie, les sociétés de prêt hypothécaire et les caisses d'épargne et de crédit" ("financial institutions which accept deposits from the public although they do not hold a charter issued pursuant to the *Bank Act*. Nearbanks include mainly trust companies, mortgage loan companies and savings and loan banks") (Canada, Department of Finance, *supra*, n. 3, p. 8).

25. McDonald, *supra*, n. 18, p. 175. See also the remarks of Mr. Justice Beetz in the decision in *Canadian Pioneer Management Ltd.*, *supra*, n. 18, pp. 449 and 450. McDonald's article was described by Mr. Justice Beetz as being "to the best of my knowledge, the most exhaustive study published on the question" (ibid., p. 455).

26. [1894] A.C. 31, p. 46.

27. [1947] A.C. 503, pp. 516 and 517.

28. See the *Canadian Pioneer Management* case, *supra*, n. 18, Beetz J. at pp. 451–54; see also McDonald, *supra*, n. 18, p. 164 et seq., p. 198; Daniel J. Baum, "The New Banks: Trust Companies of Canada" (1971), 45 *Tulane Law Review* 546; and Quebec, Comité d'étude sur les institutions financières, *supra*, n. 21, pp. 24–29.

29. P.W. Hogg, *Constitutional Law of Canada* (Toronto: Carswell, 1977), p. 367, n. 97.

30. *Canadian Pioneer Management Ltd.* decision, *supra*, n. 18, p. 451; see also, Canada, Department of Finance, *supra*, n. 4, pp. 36–38.

31. Canada, Department of Insurance, *Working Document on the Revision of the Trust Companies Act and the Loan Companies Act* (Ottawa: The Department, 1982), pp. 17 and 18.

32. Ontario, Ministry of Consumer and Commercial Relations, *Proposals for Revision of the Loan and Trust Corporation Legislation and Administration in Ontario* (Toronto: The Ministry, 1983), p. 28.

33. [1938] S.C.R. 100, Duff J. at p. 124 and Kerwin J at pp. 155 and 156.

34. [1946] A.C. 33, p. 44.

35. Decision in *Canadian Pioneer Management Ltd.*, *supra*, n. 18, pp. 449, 458, 461 and 470. "All things considered, I don't think it is possible, at least for the purpose of the present government, to define banking operations in purely functional terms." (Beetz, p. 461) An analysis of the legal content of the concept of "banking business" is found in C.C. Johnston, "Judicial Comment on the Concept of 'Banking Business'" (1962), 2 *Osgoode Hall L.J.* 347. In general, see also François Chevrette and Herbert Marx, *Droit Constitutionnel* (Montreal: Presses de l'Université de Montréal, 1982), pp. 604 and 605.

36. *Banks and Banking Law Revision Act, 1980*, S.C. 1980–81, c. 40, part 1, *Bank Act*, s. 2(1) "Banks," pp. 3 and 310; see also *Interpretation Act*, R.S.C. 1970, c. 1-23, s. 20(3). It is most interesting to note that although Parliament did not feel that it was appropriate, at the level of local financial institutions, to give "banks" the exclusive right to accept deposits transferable by cheque, it did not hesitate to use this test to subject foreign banks to its banking legislation. In fact, s. 303 of the *Bank Act* provides that non-bank affiliates of foreign banking groups shall not "engage in the business of both lending money and accepting deposit liabilities transferable by cheque or other instrument" (*Banks and Banking Law Revision Act, 1980*, S.C. 1980, c. 40, s. 303).

37. Decision in *Canadian Pioneer Management Ltd.*, *supra*, n. 18, pp. 441 and 463.

38. Ibid., pp. 468 and 469.

39. F.J.E. Jordan, *Privacy, Computer Data Banks Communications and the Constitution*. Study prepared for the Privacy and Computer Task Force (Ottawa: Department of Communications, Department of Justice, 1972), p. 9. It should, however, be noted that Parliament's jurisdiction over data processing could come under other heads in the *Constitution Act, 1867* — for example, undertakings or companies involved in interprovincial transportation or communications. The Canadian Parliament requires that Canadian banks keep on Canadian soil the books and records required or authorized by the *Bank Act* [*Banks and Banking Law Revision Act, 1980*, S.C. 1980–81, c. 40, s. 157(4)]; see, with regard to foreign banks, s. 269(1)(i).

40. See, for example, the decisions in *Bank of Toronto v. Lambe* (1887), 12 App. Cas. 575; *Re Alberta Statutes*, [1938] S.C.R. 100; *A.-G. Alberta v. A.-G. Canada* (case on the taxation of banks), [1939] A.C. 117; *A.-G. Canada v. A.-G. Quebec* (case on bank deposits), [1947] A.C. 33; as well as the decision in *Canadian Pioneer Management Ltd.*, *supra*, n. 18, p. 469, Hogg, *supra*, n. 29, p. 366; and Chevrette and Marx, *supra*, n. 35, pp. 605–607.

41. As regards the commerce clause, see A. Smith, *The Commerce Power in Canada and in the United States* (Toronto: Butterworth, 1963); P.W. Hutchins and P.J. Kenniff, "The Concept of Interstate Commerce" (1969), 10 *Cahiers de droit* 705; Nicole Dupré, "A propos de l'affaire Pilote : les pouvoirs provinciaux en matière de réglementation du commerce" (1974), 15 *Cahiers de droit* 568; André Tremblay, "Chronique — vers une impossible définition de l'article 91(2) du BNA Act" (1971), 31 *Revue du Barreau* 112; André Tremblay, "L'affaire des oeufs ou le triomphe du marché commun canadien" (1971), 31 *Revue du Barreau* 469; O. Bourque, "L'affaire des omelettes et ses conséquences sur le partage des compétences législatives en matière de taxation et de commerce" (1978), 19 *Cahiers de droit* 1115; Leavy, *supra*, n. 2; James C. MacPherson, "Economic Regulation and the British North America Act" (1980–81), 5 *Can. Bus. L.J.* 172; Finkelstein, "Notes of Cases" (1984), 62 *Can. Bar Rev.* 182; Chevrette and Marx, *supra*, n. 35, pp. 431–24.

42. (1881) 7 App. Cas. 96. A summary of the case-law which applies to the first aspect of the Parsons case is found in Mr. Justice Estey's remarks, in *Labatt Breweries of Canada Ltd. v. A.-G. Canada*, [1980] 1 S.C.R. 914, pp. 936–44; 30 N.R. 496, pp. 514–20.

43. Leavy, *supra*, n. 2, p. 17 and 18; MacPherson, *supra*, n. 41, p. 174 et seq. The

restrictive approach to the commerce clause adopted by the courts during this period was the subject of some harsh comments; see F.R. Scott, "Centralization and Decentralization in Canadian Federalism," (1951), 29 *Can. Bar Rev.* 1095; V. MacDonald, "The Constitution in a Changing World" (1948), 26 *Can. Bar Rev.* 21; William F. O'Connor, parliamentary advisor, *Report Relating to the British North America Act, 1867,* Report to the Canadian Senate, Ottawa, 1939. The second aspect of the Parsons case has been applied by the Privy Council on only two occasions:

a) in *John Deere Plow Co. v. Wharton,* [1915] A.C. 330; (1914) 18 D.L.R. 353; 7 W.W.R. 706 with regard to certain aspects of the incorporation of federal companies;

b) in *A.-G. Ontario v. A.-G. Canada,* [1937] A.C. 405; (1937) D.L.R. 702; 67 C.C.C. 342; [1937] W.W.R. 333 with regard to federal trademark legislation.

Generally speaking, the existence of the general power to regulate commerce was rejected during this period (see Hogg, *supra,* n. 29, pp. 272 and 273). Among other things, the case law has firmly established that the second aspect of the Parsons case does not allow Parliament to regulate a specific business (see the summary of the case law on this point by Mr. Justice Estey in *Labatt Breweries Ltd, supra,* n. 42, pp. 517 and 518 and the comments of Dickson in *R. v. Wetmore,* [1983] 2 S.C.R. 284, p. 294.

44. *Alberta Statutes Reference,* [1938] S.C.R. 100, p. 116; pp. 120 and 121 by Duff J., Davis and Hudson concurring (pp. 162 and 163). See the comments by Mr. Justice Dickson in *A.-G. Canada v. Canadian National Transportation Ltd.,* [1983] 2 S.C.R. 206, p. 259.

45. Chrétien, *supra,* n. 2, p. 24; MacPherson, *supra,* n. 41, p. 185.

46. See the comments of Chief Justice Dickson describing the situation with respect to the second aspect of s. 91(2) of the Canadian Constitution in the case of *A.-G. Canada v. Canadian National Transportation Ltd,* [1983] 2 S.C.R. 206, pp. 261–68. The majority decision, rendered by the Supreme Court sitting with seven judges, was handed down by Chief Justice Laskin (Ritchie, Estey and McIntyre JJ concurring), who recognized the right of the Attorney-General of Canada to institute proceedings of a criminal nature directly by virtue of the (federal) *Combines Investigation Act.* Chief Justice Laskin did not deem it appropriate to comment on whether or not the commerce clause was applicable in such circumstances. However, Mr. Justice Dickson (Beetz and Lamer JJ concurring) upheld the constitutionality of the (federal) *Combines Investigation Act* on the basis of s. 91(27) of the *Constitution Act, 1867* and he concluded that the second aspect of the Parsons case was valid and applicable. He summarizes the applicable criteria as follows:

> In approaching this difficult problem of characterization, it is useful to note the remarks of the Chief Justice in *MacDonald v. Vapor Can. Ltd.,* [1977], 2 S.C.R. 134, at 165, in which he cites as possible indicia for a valid exercise of the general trade and commerce power the presence of a national regulatory scheme, the oversight of a regulatory agency and a concern with trade in general rather than with an aspect of a particular business. To this list I would add what to my mind would be even stronger indications of valid general regulation of trade and commerce, namely (i) that the provinces jointly or severally would be constitutionally incapable of passing such an enactment and (ii) that failure to include one or more provinces or localities would jeopardize successful operation in other parts of the country.
>
> The above does not purport to be an exhaustive list, nor is the presence of any or all of these indicia necessarily decisive. The proper approach to the characterization is still the one suggested in *Parsons,* a careful case-by-case assessment. Nevertheless, the presence of such factors does at least make it far more probable that what is being addressed in a federal enactment is genuinely a national economic concern and not just a collection of local ones (ibid., pp. 267 and 268).

See also Neil Finkelstein, "Notes of Cases" (1984), 62 *Can. Bar Rev.* 182; and the comments of Chief Justice Laskin in *MacDonald v. Vapor Can. Ltd.*

47. Although there has been no formal statement to this effect, it would seem that we can assume that the Supreme Court, when referring to s. 91(2) of the *Constitution Act, 1867,* meant the second aspect of the *Parsons* decision. Professor Hogg considers it to

belong to the second aspect of *Parsons*. (See P.W. Hogg, "The Constitutionality of Federal Regulation of Mutual Funds," in J.C. Baillie and W.M.H. Grover (eds.), *Proposals for a Mutual Fund Law for Canada* (Ottawa: Information Canada, 1974), vol. 1, p. 83). See also Mr. Justice Dickson's remarks with respect to the Alberta Statutes Reference in *A.-G. Canada v. Canadian National Transportation Ltd*, [1983] 2 S.C.R. 206, p. 259.

48. P. Anisman and P. W. Hogg, "Constitutional Aspects of Federal Securities Legislation" in Canada, Department of Consumer and Corporate Affairs, *Proposals for a Securities Market Law for Canada*, vol. 3, *Background Papers* (Ottawa: Minister of Supply and Services Canada, 1979), pp. 166–71.

49. [1982] 2 S.C.R. 161, Dickson at p. 173, and Estey at pp. 224 and 225.

50. See Philip Anisman, "The Proposals for a Securities Market Law for Canada: Purpose and Process" (1981), 19 *Osgoode Hall L. J.* 329, 352, 359 and 360. Canadian Bar Association, *supra*, n. 2, p. 111.

51. Anisman, *supra*, n. 50, pp. 365–67. It would seem, however, that inasmuch as the validity of a federal securities statute relies upon the federal government's general power of economic regulation, the government could control intraprovincial transactions.

52. Hogg, *supra*, n. 47, pp. 82–85 and 87.

53. Robert A. Donaldson, "Foreign Investment Review and Canadianization" (1982), *Special Lectures, Law Society of Upper Canada* 461, at p. 477; see also Hogg, *supra*, n. 29, p. 315.

54. [1978] 2 S.C.R. 545, Martland J. at pp. 568 and 569. Mr. Justice Martland expressed his concerns with regard to the real effect of the fiscal measures enacted by Saskatchewan as follows:

> The practical consequence of the application of this legislation is that the Government of Saskatchewan will acquire the benefit of all increases in the value of oil produced in that Province above the set basic well-head price fixed by the statute and regulations, which is approximately the same as that which existed in 1973 before the increase in world prices for oil. In this connection, there is the important fact that 98 percent of all crude oil produced in Saskatchewan is destined for export from the Province either to Eastern Canada or the United States of America. (ibid., p. 557).

It should, however, be noted that the *ratio decidendi* of the remarks of Mr. Justice Martland (speaking for the majority) was not aimed at the process of the accumulation of capital but at the unconstitutionality of provincial measures establishing selling prices for goods on export markets (ibid., p. 568). In addition, the court referred, in this case, to the usual test for applying the first aspect of the commerce clause, which, as we have mentioned, probably only covers the movement of goods (Chrétien, *supra*, n. 2, p. 24; MacPherson, *supra*, n. 41, p. 185). With regard to the movement of capital, it is in fact the criterion of the applicability of the general power of economic regulation (second aspect in the *Parsons* case) which must be met.

55. As regards the constitutional power to legislate for "peace, order and good government," see, among others, Hogg, *supra*, n. 29, pp. 241–65; Patrick N. McDonald, "Peace, Order and Good Government: The Laskin Court in the Anti-Inflation Act Reference" (1977), 23 *McGill Law Journal* 431; MacPherson, *supra*, n. 41, pp. 177–99; P. Hogg, "Comment on James C. MacPhersons's Paper on Economic Regulation and the British North America Act" (1980–1981), 5 *Can. Bus. L. J.* 172, pp. 221 and 222; W.R. Lederman, "Unity and Diversity in Canadian Federalism: Ideals and Methods of Moderation" (1975), 53 *Can. Bar Rev.* 596, at p. 603; Bora Laskin, "Peace, Order and Good Government Reexamined" (1947), 25 *Can. Bar Rev.* 1054; Gibson, "Measuring National Dimensions" (1976), 7 *Man. L. J.* 15; Anisman and Hogg, *supra*, n. 48, pp. 177–86; Chevrette and Marx, *supra*, n. 35, pp. 427–29.

56. *Citizen's Insurance Company of Canada v. Parsons* (1881) 1 App. Cas. 96; and *Jones v. A.-G. New Brunswick*, [1975] 2 S.C.R. 182.

57. [1976] 2 S.C.R. 373, pp. 427, 437, 461 and 467. See Hogg, *supra*, n. 29, pp. 248–57.

58. *Reference re Anti-Inflation Act*, [1976] 2 S.C.R. 373, Beetz J. at pp. 442–59, followed

by de Grandpré J. (p. 440), Martland, Pigeon and Ritchie JJ (p. 437); *R. v. Hauser,* [1979] 1 S.C.R. 984, p. 1000, Pigeon J.; *Labatt Breweries of Canada Ltd. v. A.-G. Canada,* [1980] 1 S.C.R. 914, p. 945 citing Hogg, supra, n. 29, pp. 259–61; *Reference re Exported National Gas Tax,* [1982] 1 S.C.R. 1004, pp. 1041 and 1042, in which the dissenting judges (McIntyre, Lamer and Laskin) held that the federal government's policy of "energy equalization" transcended the matters listed in s. 92 of the *Constitution Act, 1867.* Mr. Justice Martland, speaking for the majority, made no formal comment on the application of the "peace, order and good government" clause to the case and simply dismissed the federal government's argument; *R. v. Wetmore,* [1983] 2 S.C.R. 284, Dickson J. at pp. 274–95; *Schneider v. A.-G. British Columbia* [1983] 43 N.R. 91, pp. 110 and 111.

59. *Anti-Inflation Act,* S.C. 1974–1975, 1976, c. 75, ss. 2 and 3c). See, for example, *National Emergency Transitional Powers Act,* 1945, S.C. 1945, c. 25; and *The Continuation of Transitional Measures Act,* 1947, S.C. 1947, c. 16.

60. Anisman and Hogg, *supra,* n. 48, pp. 185–87.

61. "I agree, of course, that the mere desire for uniformity cannot be a support for an exercise of federal general power. Uniformity is almost invariably involved in federal legislation." Laskin C.J. in *Reference re Anti-Inflation Act,* [1976] 2 S.C.R. 373, p. 400.

62. In *Reference Re Insurance Act,* 1910, [1914] 48 S.C.R. 260 (see the remarks of Mr. Justice Duff at p. 304) upheld by the Privy Council, *A.-G. Canada v. A.-G. Alberta,* [1916] A.C. 588, p. 597. See also *Reference re Anti-Inflation Act,* [1976] 2 S.C.R. 373, pp. 446 and 447. See Jacques Clément, "Les pouvoirs respectifs des gouvernements fédéral et provinciaux en matière d'assurance" (1977), 45 *Assurances* 83; Hogg, *supra,* n. 29, pp. 298–302; Gérald A. Beaudoin, *Le partage des pouvoirs* (Ottawa: Éditions de l'Université d'Ottawa, 1980), p. 154.

63. See *Canadian Pioneer Management Ltd., supra,* n. 18, Laskin J. at p. 438 and Beetz J. at pp. 412–44.

64. See the excellent paper by Yves Ouellette on this issue, Yves Ouellette, "Le partage des compétences en matière de constitution des sociétés" (1980–1981) 15 *Revue juridique Thémis* 113.

    Professor Yves Ouellette has provided a convincing explanation of the theoretical confusion resulting from the Lord Haldane's suggestions in *John Deere Plow Company Ltd. v. Wharton* (1915), A.C. 330, p. 340, to the effect that the commerce clause justifies the regulation by Parliament of the powers of a company which it has incorporated (ibid., pp. 126–29).

    The real impact of this confusion is that in every case, it gives legislative predominance to the federal government's power to incorporate companies over the enumerated powers of legislative assemblies; yet Parliament ought to benefit only in cases where the exercise of that power is related to one of the powers enumerated. The Quebec Court of Appeal, in *Montel v. Groupe de Consultants P.G.L. Inc.* [(1982) 142 D.L.R. (3d) 659] quoting Dickson J. in the *Multiple Access* case, upheld Parliament's right to encroach on provincial powers without regard to the conditions upon which the incorporation of a given federal company is based (p. 674 et seq.).

65. *Kootenay and Elk Railway Co. v. Canadian Pacific Railway,* [1974] S.C.R. 955; (1972) 28 D.L.R. (3d) 385, Laskin J. at pp. 427 and 428; see also *Canadian Pioneer Management Ltd., supra,* n. 18, Laskin J. at pp. 439 and 440, and Beetz J. at p. 463.

66. See, among others, *Rathie v. Montreal Trust Co.* (1952) G.W.W.R. (N.S.) 652; *Lakey and Ruthenian Farmers' Elevator Co.,* [1924] S.C.R. 56, p. 72; *A.-G. Manitoba v. A.-G. Canada,* [1929] A.C. 260, pp. 266 and 267; *Reference re Constitutional Validity of s. 110 of the Dominion Companies Act,* [1934] S.C.R. 653, p. 658; *Multiple Access Ltd. v. McCutcheon,* [1982] 2 S.C.R. 161, pp. 176–79; 44 N.R. 181, (Dickson) at pp. 197–99 and [Estey (dissenting)] at p. 200; *Doyle v. Restrictive Trade Practices Commission and Sparling* (1984) 51 N.R. 223 (F.C.A.); *Montel v. Groupe de consultants P.G.L. Inc.,* (1982) 142 D.L.R. (3d) 659; *Esso Standard (Inter-American) Inc. v. J.W. Enterprises Inc.,* [1963] S.C.R. 144, Mr. Justice Judson at p. 152 citing Professor J.A. Laidlaw; Hogg, *supra,* n. 29, p. 353; Chevrette and Marx, *supra,* n. 35, pp. 567–73.

67. *Canadian Indemnity Ltd. v. A.-G. British Columbia*, [1976] 2 S.C.R. 503.

68. *Great West Sadderly v. R.*, [1921] A.C. 91; *Morgan v. A.-G. Prince Edward Island*, [1976] S.C.R. 349.

69. *Lymburn v. Mayland*, [1932] A.C. 318.

70. *Société Asbestos Ltée v. Société nationale de l'amiante*, [1981] Quebec C.A. 43, p. 51 (permission to appeal to the Supreme Court refused).

71. Supreme Court of Canada, May 3, 1984, comments of Mr. Justice McIntyre at pp. 35–44 (unanimous decision of the court) (sub. nom. *Re Upper Churchill Water Rights Reservation Act*, 1 R.S.C. 297.

72. Ibid., p. 325.

73. *Investment Companies Act*, S.C. 1970–1971, 1972, c. 33, s. 2(1), "company" and "investment company," and s. 3.

74. *Canada Business Corporations Act*, S.C. 1974–1975, c. 33, s. 100(3).

75. Ibid., s. 31(1), as added by S.C 1980–1981, 1982, c. 115, s. 2.

76. See, among others, *National Energy Board Act*, R.C.S. 1970, c. N-6, as amended, s. 2, "Company," 25 and 63; *Telesat Canada Act*, R.S.C. 1970, c. T-4, as amended; *National Transportation Act*, R.S.C., 1970, c. N-17, as amended, s. 29, "Company," 30 and 34 (commodity pipeline); s. 36 [Extraprovincial motor vehicle transport (any person may apply for a licence)]; *Aeronautics Act*, R.S.C. 1970, c. A-3, as amended, s. 16(1) (any person may apply for a licence), but 15/1 and 16(2) impose strict controls on share transfers; *Air Canada Act, 1971*, S.C. 1976–1977, c. 5; Railway Act, R.S.C. 1970, c. R-2, as amended; *Teleglobe Canada Act*, R.S.C. 1970, c. C-11, as amended; *Broadcasting Act*, R.S.C. 1970, c. B-11, as amended: *Telegraphs Act*, R.S.C. 1970, c. T-3, as amended.

77. *An Act to limit shareholding in certain corporations*, Bill S-31 (1st reading, November 2, 1982), 1st session, 32nd Parliament (Can.), s. 3 et seq.

78. See the testimony of Pierre Lortie, chairman of the Montreal Stock Exchange, before the Senate Standing Committee on Legal and Constitutional Affairs, *Proceedings on the Subject-Matter of Bill S-31*, November 30, 1982.

79. See Joan G. Fickinger, "Jurisdiction of State Regulatory Commissions over Public Utility Holding Company Diversification" (1983), 15 *Loyola University of Chicago Law Journal*; *Utility Diversification Strategies and Issues* (New York: Public Utilities Reports, The Management Exchange, 1981).

80. See, generally, Nicolas Roy, "The TransQuebec and Maritimes Pipeline Project: The Jurisdictional Debate in the Area of Land Planning" (1982), 23 *Cahiers de droit* 175, pp. 186–95.

81. Hogg, *supra*, n. 47, p. 83.

82. Ontario, Ministry of Consumer and Commercial Relations, *supra*, n. 32, p. 22.

83. *Constitution Act, 1867*, 30–31 Victoria, c. 3 (U.K.), s. 132. Section 132 deals with the internal enforcement of international obligations agreed to by the imperial government. In fact, s. 132 enables Parliament to legislate with respect to the enforcement of obligations arising from imperial treaties even in a case where the legislation in question is related to matters within provincial jurisdiction (see Anne-Marie Jacomy-Millette, *Introduction et application des traités internationaux au Canada* (Paris: Librairie générale de droit et de jurisprudence, 1971), pp. 231–38.

84. A summary of the historical events linked to the development of Canada's international personality is found in Jacomy-Millette, *supra*, n. 83, pp. 5–45. In Canada, jurisdiction to enter into international agreements belongs to the Crown, through the rights and powers of the royal prerogative; however, the exercise of these rights and powers by the federal or provincial authorities remains in dispute (ibid., pp. 49–96). As far as external affairs and international agreements are concerned, see, generally, Chevrette and Marx, *supra*, n. 35, pp. 1194–99.

85. *A.-G. Canada v. A.-G. Ontario* (*Labour Conventions* case), [1937] A.C. 326; see, generally, Jacomy-Millette, *supra*, n. 83, pp. 171–240 and 351. See, generally, Hogg, *supra*, n. 29, pp. 189–93; J. Brossard, A. Patry and E. Weiser, *Les pouvoirs extérieurs*

*du Québec* (Montreal: Presses de l'Université de Montréal, 1967), K.C. Wheare, *Federal Government*, 4th ed. (London: Greenwood Press, 1963), chap. 9.

86. [1977] 2 S.C.R. 134, p. 171. Mr. Justice Laskin has suggested that two tests are sufficient to determine the validity of federal legislation which gives effect to an international treaty:

a) the legislation under examination should explain clearly the legislature's intention to give effect to a treaty;

b) the legislation must not exceed the scope of the treaty or the convention.

87. Schneider v. R., [1982] 2 S.C.R. 112, pp. 134–35. See the strong criticism by A.L.C. de Mestral with respect to the potential scope of Mr. Justice Dickson's remarks on the balance of powers of Parliament and the provinces with respect to the enforcement of treaties (A.L.C. de Mestral, "Treaty-Power, and More on Rules and Obiter Dicta" (1983), 61 *Can. Bar Rev.* 856).

88. E.J. Arnett, "Canadian Regulation of Foreign Investment: The Legal Parameters" (1972), 50 *Can. Bar Rev.* 213, at p. 244. A legal and historic outline of the issue of the liberalization of international capital movements is found in Pierre Jasinski, *Régime juridique de la circulation des capitaux* (Paris: Librarie générale de droit et de jurisprudence, 1967).

89. The Code of Liberalization of Capital Movements was adopted by the Council of the Organisation for Economic Co-operation and Development (OECD) on December 12, 1961 (OECD/C (1961)96) and amended on several subsequent occasions (hereafter designated as the "code").

   The OECD has published analyses demonstrating the degree to which member states (including Canada, although it does not abide by the code) conform to the code's provisions; see OECD, *Controls on International Capital Movements — Experience with Controls on International Financial Credits, Loans and Deposits* (Paris: OECD, 1982); OECD, *Controls and Impediments Affecting Inward Direct Investments in OECD Member Countries* (Paris: OECD, 1982).

90. See B.S. Fisher and R.G. Steinhardt III, "Section 301 of the Trade Act of 1974: Protection for U.S. Exporters of Goods, Services, and Capital" (1982), 14 *Law & Pol'y in Int'l Bus.* 569, pp. 679 and 680.

91. Code, *supra*, n. 89, appendix C, "Decision of the Council Regarding the Application of the Provisions of the Code of Liberalization of Capital Movements to Action Taken by States of the United States."

92. OECD, "Annex to the Declarations of 21st June, 1976 by Governments of OECD Member Countries on International Investment and Multinational Enterprises" (Paris: OECD, 1976).

   OECD, *International Investment and Multinational Enterprises* (Paris: OECD, 1976). The document includes the "Declaration on International Investment and Multinational Enterprises" to which the "Guidelines for Multinational Enterprises" and three decisions of the council of the OECD are attached; see Fisher and Steinhardt III, *supra*, n. 90, pp. 681 and 682.

93. David Stewart-Patterson, "GATT Report on FIRA Is Generally Favourable," *Globe and Mail*, January 21, 1984, p. RB-19. GATT Panel Report, *Canada — Administration of Foreign Investment Review Act*, file L/5504 cited in E.J. Arnett, R. Rueter, and E.P. Mendes, "FIRA and the Rule of Law" (1984), 62 *Can. Bar Rev.* 121, p. 122, n. 4.

94. Knopper, *supra*, n. 22, pp. 9–11; James R. Basche Jr., *Regulating International Data Transmission*, report no. 852 (Ottawa: Conference Board of Canada, 1984).

95. See discussion paper based on the work of the International Task Force on Transborder Data Flows, September 1983. As regards the Canadian position with respect to the international exchange of date, see W.H. Montgomery, *Transborder Data Flow, Canadian Directions*, a keynote address to the OECD Symposium on Transborder Data Flow, London, November 30, 1983. On this subject, see "Les flux transfrontières de données — les problèmes qu'ils soulèvent — le bilan de leur utilisation" in *Problèmes politiques et sociaux — la documentation française*, November 30, 1984.

96. OECD, *Lignes directrices régissant la protection de la vie privé et les flux transfrontières de donnés de caractère personnel* (Paris: OECD, 1981).

97. The powers of taxation of the legislative assemblies and of Parliament have been the subject of a good deal of doctrinal writing: see, inter alia, G.V. La Forest, *The Allocation of Taxing Power Under the Canadian Constitution*, 2nd ed. (Toronto: Canadian Tax Foundation, 1981); J.N. Lyon and Ronald G. Atkey, *Canadian Constitutional Law in a Modern Perspective* (Toronto: University of Toronto Press, 1970), pp. 1058–94; John D. Whyte and W.R. Lederman, *Canadian Constitutional Law*, 2nd ed. (Toronto: Butterworth, 1977), chap. 9; Bora Laskin, *Canadian Constitutional Law*, 4th ed. (Toronto: Carswell, 1975), chap. 12; Hogg, *supra*, n. 29, chap. 23; Chevrette and Marx, *supra*, n. 35, pp. 1064–76.

98. *Re Insurance Act of Canada*, [1932] A.C. 41, p. 52; *Reference re Agricultural Products Marketing Act*, [1978] 2 S.C.R. 1198, pp. 1233 and 1234. See, generally, La Forest, *supra*, n. 97, pp. 41–45.

99. *Reference re Anti-Inflation Act*, [1976] 2 S.C.R. 373, Laskin J. at p. 390; *Reference re Exported Natural Gas Tax*, [1982] 1 S.C.R. 1004; [1982] 5 W.W.R. 577. See, on this decision, William D. Mouli, "Commentary — Alberta Natural Gas Referece: Effect on Public Enterprise in Canada" (1982–1983), 7 *Can. Bus. L. J.* 485; La Forest, *supra*, n. 97, pp. 182–86.

100. See Marc Lalonde, *Research and Development Tax Policies* (Ottawa: Department of Finance, 1983); Marc Lalonde, *Building Better Pensions for Canadians* (Ottawa: Department of Finance, 1984); and Canada, Department of Finance, *Action Plan for Pension Reform* (Ottawa: The Department, 1984).

101. Thomas J. Courchene, "The National Energy Program and Fiscal Federalism: Some Observations," in G.C. Watkins and M.A. Walker (eds.), *Reaction: The National Energy Program* (Vancouver: Fraser Institute, 1981), pp. 94 and 95.

102. Alberta, Government of Alberta White Paper, *Proposals for an Industrial and Science Strategy for Albertans 1985 to 1990* (Edmonton, July 1984), p. 62 and 63.

103. Arnett, *supra*, n. 88, pp. 214–31. Arnett's article was published before the *Foreign Investment Review Act* was passed.

104. *Foreign Investment Review Act*, S.C. 1973–1974, c. 46, as amended; Donaldson, *supra*, n. 53, pp. 476 and 477.

   On December 7, 1984, the Minister of Industry, Sinclair Stevens, filed Bill C-15 (*Investment Canada Act*), whose object is to create Investment Canada to replace the Foreign Investment Review Agency.

   A critical assessment of the Foreign Investment Review Agency is found in Christopher C. Beckman, *The Foreign Investment Review Agency: Images and Realities*, study no. 84 (Ottawa: Conference Board of Canada, 1984); Arnett, et al., *supra*, n. 93.

105. *Smith v. R.*, [1960] S.C.R. 776. See also the decision in *Labatt Breweries of Canada*, *supra*, n. 42, pp. 511 and 512.

106. Reference as to the Validity of Section 5(a) of the *Dairy Industry Act* (margarine reference), [1949] S.C.R. 1, Rand J. at p. 50 affirmed by [1951] A.C. 179.

107. Anisman and Hogg, *supra*, n. 48, pp. 187–89.

108. Welling, *supra*, n. 22, p. 18; Jordan, *supra*, n. 39, pp. 16 and 17. In February 1984, the federal minister of justice tabled Bill C-19, *Criminal Law Reform Act, 1984*, which included provisions relating to computer crime [*Criminal Law Reform Act, 1984*, Bill C-19 (1st reading), 2nd session, 32nd Parliament (Can.), s. 88]. Bill C-19 died on the order paper when Parliament was adjourned in July 1984. The Conservative government that was elected on September 4, 1984, introduced a similar bill on December 19, 1984 [*Criminal Law Amendment Act, 1984*, Bill C-18 (1st reading), 1st session, 33rd Parliament (Can.), ss. 45 and 58].

109. See Roy, *supra*, n. 80; Gil Rémillard, *Le fédéralisme canadien* (Montreal: Québec/Amérique, 1980), pp. 309–43; I.H. Fraser, "Some Comments on Subsection 92(10) of the Constitution Act, 1867" (1984), 29 *McGill L. J.* 557; Chevrette and Marx, *supra*, n. 35, pp. 915–90.

110. See, generally, as regards the declaratory power, Andrée Lajoie, *Le pouvoir déclaratoire du Parlement* (Montreal: Presses de l'Université de Montréal, 1969); Fraser, *supra*, n. 109.

111. See, generally, Stanley Goldstein, *Changing Times: Banking in the Electronic Age* (Ottawa: Minister of Supply and Services Canada, 1979).

112. Welling, *supra*, n. 22, pp. 14 and 15.

113. Ibid., p. 16. A detailed discussion of the division of responsibilities between Parliament and the legislative assemblies with regard to computer networks and data used in automated teller machines and other similar systems is found in Jordan, *supra*, n. 39, pp. 42–64.

On technical developments in the financial sector, see H.H. Binhammer and Jane Williams, *L'innovation dans les institutions de dépôts*, study prepared for the Economic Council of Canada (Ottawa: Minister of Supply and Services Canada, 1977); Richard Skimlis, "A Free-for-all in ATMs?" *Financial Times*, September 10, 1984, pp. 13 and 14; Robert Taylor, "Access Seeks Firms for ATMs," *Globe and Mail*, September 19, 1984, p. RB-7.

114. Anisman, *supra*, n. 50, pp. 335, 356 and 357.

115. Pierre Lortie, president of the Montreal Stock Exchange, "The Montreal Exchange: The Challenge of the Eighties," speech given to the Canadian Club of Montreal, October 29, 1984. The Toronto Stock Exchange uses the CATS system (Computer Assisted Trading System) whereas the Montreal Stock Exchange introduced a more sophisticated system for its operations, the MORRE (Montreal Exchange Registered Representative Order Routing and Execution System). See, generally, with regard to the technical aspects of the automation of securities transactions, Hugh J. Cleland, "Applications of Automation in the Canadian Securities Industry: Present and Projected" in Canada, Department of Consumer and Corporate Affairs, *Proposals for a Securities Market Law for Canada*, vol. 3, *Background Papers* (Ottawa: Minister of Supply and Services Canada), 1979, pp. 947–1056; Michael A. Jenkins, "Computer Communications Systems in Securities Markets" in Canada, Department of Consumer and Corporate Affairs, *Proposals for a Securities Market Law for Canada*, vol. 3, *Background Papers* (Ottawa: Minister of Supply and Services Canada, 1979), pp. 1057–1138; J. Peter Williamson, "Canadian Capital Markets" in Canada, Department of Consumer and Corporate Affairs, *Proposals for a Securities Market Law*, vol. 3, *Background Papers* (Ottawa: Minister of Supply and Services Canada, 1979), pp. 124–28; G.M. Hawley, "Central Depository System for Securities" (1982–1983), 7 *Can. Bus. L. J.* 306; Knoppers, *supra*, n. 22, p. 44.

116. See Ouellette, *supra*, n. 64.

117. The federal government's spending power is implictly based on its power over taxation [s. 91(3)] and public property [s. 91(1A)], on its legislative power to legislative for the "peace, order and good government of Canada" (preamble to s. 91), on its authority over the Consolidated Revenue Fund (ss. 102 and 106), on the royal prerogative and on common law. See, generally, J. Dupont, "Le pouvoir de dépenser du gouvernement fédéral: "A Dead Issue" (1967), *U.B.C. L. Rev. — Cahiers de droit* 69; Jean Beetz, "Les attitudes changeantes du Québec à l'endroit de la Constitution de 1867," in P.A. Crépeau and C.B. MacPherson (eds.), *L'avenir du fédéralism canadien* (Toronto and Montreal: University of Toronto Press/Presses de l'Université de Montréal, 1965), p. 129; Chevrette and Marx, *supra*, n. 35, pp. 1039–48; J.E. Magnet, "The Constitutional Distribution of Taxation Powers in Canada" (1978), 10 *Ottawa L. Rev.* 473, pp. 480 and 481; P.E. Trudeau, "Les Octrois fédéraux aux universités," in *Le fédéralisme et la société canadienne-française* (Montreal: Éditions H.M.H., 1967); P.E. Trudeau, *Les subventions fédérales-provinciales et le pouvoir de dépenser du Parlement canadien* (Ottawa: Queen's Printer, 1969); E.A. Driedger, "The Spending Power" (1981), 7 *Queen's L. J.* 124; Hogg, *supra*, n. 29, p. 69 et seq.; F.R. Scott, "The Constitutional Background of Taxation Agreements" (1955), 2 *McGill L.J.* 1; Donald V. Smiley and Ronald M. Burns, "Canadian Federalism and the Spending Power" (1969), 17 *Canadian Tax Journal* 468. See also Allan Tupper, *Public Money in the Private Sector* (Kingston: Queen's University, Institute of Intergovernmental Relations, 1982), Economic Council of Canada, *supra*, n. 8.

118. *A.-G. Canada v. A.-G. Ontario*, [1937] A.C. 355, pp. 366 and 367 (by Lord Atkin). See Andrée Lajoie, *Contrats administratifs — jalons pour une théorie* (Montreal: Les Éditions Thémis, 1984), pp. 141–68.

119. Andrée Lajoie, "Nouvelle offensive du pouvoir fédéral de dépenser," *Le Devoir*, March 6, 1984, p. 1; and "L'éducation — nouvelle offensive du pouvoir fédéral de dépenser — 2," *Le Devoir*, March 7, 1984, p. 7; Lajoie, *supra*, n. 118, pp. 116–18.

120. Economic Council of Canada, *supra*, n. 8, Canada, Department of Energy, Mines and Resources, *National Energy Programme, 1980* (Ottawa: Minister of Supply and Services Canada, 1980), p. 41 et seq.

121. *Constitution Act, 1867*, 30–31 Victoria, c. 3 (U.K.), ss. 91(1A) and 91(4).

122. *A.-G. Ontario v. Policy Holders of Wentworth Insurance Co.*, [1969] S.C.R. 779.

123. Hogg, *supra*, n. 29, pp. 301 and 302; Anisman and Hogg, *supra*, n. 48, p. 170.

124. S.C. 1970–1971, c. 33, s. 2(1), (9).

125. *British North America Act* (1951), 14–15 George VI, c. 32 (U.K.), as repealed and replaced by *the Constitution Act of 1964*, 12–13 Eliz. II, c. 73 (U.K.); see Hogg, *supra*, n. 29, pp. 223–25. With respect to pension funds, see, generally, Neufeld, *supra*, n. 21, p. 442–57; D.E. Bond and R.A. Shearer, *The Economics of the Canadian Financial System* (Toronto: Prentice Hall, 1972), pp. 242–44; Canada, Royal Commission on Corporate Concentration, *Report* (Ottawa: Minister of Supply and Services Canada, 1978), p. 267; A. Don Ezra, *The Struggle for Pension Fund Wealth* (Toronto: Pagurian Press, 1983); Economic Council of Canada, *Perspective 2030 — The Future of Retirement Pensions* (Ottawa: Minister of Supply and Services Canada, 1979); Pradeep Kumar and Alister M.M. Smith, *Pension Reform in Canada: A Review of the Issues and Problems*, Research and Current Issues Series no. 40 (Kingston: Queen's University, Industrial Relations Center, 1981); David W. Conklin, Salynn H. Bennett and Thomas J. Courchene (eds.), *Pensions Today and Tomorrow: Background Studies* (Toronto: Ontario Economic Council, 1984); Canadian Association of Pension Supervisory Authorities, *A Consensus for Pension Reform* (Ottawa: The Association, 1982).

For the federal government's position, see Marc Lalonde, *Building Better Pensions for Canadians* (Ottawa: Department of Finance, 1984), pp. 6 and 7; see also, Canada, Government of Canada, *Better Pensions for Canadians* (Ottawa, Minister of Supply and Services Canada, 1982); Canada, House of Commons, Parliamentary Task Force on Pension Reform, *Report*, 1st session, 32nd Parliament, 1983; Canada, Task Force on Retirement Income Policy, *The Retirement Income System in Canada: Problems and Alternative Policies for Reform*, 2 vols. (Ottawa: Minister of Supply and Services Canada, 1980) (Lazar Report).

126. David M. Cameron and J. Stefan Dupré, "The Financial Framework of Distribution and Social Services," in Stanley M. Beck and Ivan Bernier (eds.), *Canada and the New Constitution — The Unfinished Agenda* (Montreal: Institute for Research on Public Policy, 1983), pp. 357 and 358.

127. Keith G. Banting, "The Decision Rules: Federalism and Pension Reform," in David W. Conklin, Salynn H. Bennett and Thomas J. Courchene (eds.), *Pensions Today and Tomorrow: Background Studies* (Toronto: Ontario Economic Council, 1984), pp. 197 and 198.

128. *Canada Pension Plan Act*, R.S.C. 1970, c. C-5; see Banting, *supra*, n. 127, pp. 194–96.

129. Ibid., pp. 191, 192, 195 and 207, n. 10. This condition is probably unconstitutional, since it is contrary to the predominant right of the provinces provided for in s. 94A of the Canadian Constitution.

130. *Constitution Act, 1867*, 30–31 Victoria, c. 3 (U.K.), s. 92(13) and (16).

131. (1881) App. Cas. 96.

132. Chrétien, supra, n. 2, p. 47; see, generally, Quebec, Conseil exécutif, Comité interministériel sur les investissements étrangers, *Report, cadre et les moyens d'une politique québécoise concernant les investissements étrangers* (Quebec, 1973, revised text, March to June 1974), pp. 64, 66 and 158 (hereafter, the Tetley Report); Hogg, *supra*, n. 29, pp. 355–59.

It can be argued that s. 6 of the *Canadian Charter of Rights and Freedoms* severely limits the power of the provinces to use the licence or permit requirement as an indirect means of controlling foreign individuals or corporations (to the extent that

s. 6 deals with them, see *supra*, n. 12) which want to do business in their territory (Davies, Ward and Beck, *supra*, n. 12, pp. 26 and 27).

133. *Canadian Indemnity v. A.-G. British Columbia*, [1977] 2 S.C.R. 504.

134. See, generally, Jacques Clément, "Les pouvoirs législatifs des gouvernements fédéral et provinciaux en matière d'assurance" (1977), *Assurances* 83; Macdonald, "The Regulation of Insurance in Canada" (1946), 24 *Can. Bar Rev.* 481; Bora Laskin, *Canadian Constitutional Law*, 3rd ed. (Toronto: Carswell, 1969), p. 603; A. Smith, *supra*, n. 41, pp. 80–90; McDonald, *supra*, n. 18, pp. 166–71; Hogg, *supra*, n. 29, pp. 299–302; Chevrette and Marx, *supra*, n. 35, pp. 524–27.

135. See the exhaustive list of provincial legislative provisions prepared on these points by Professor Ivan Bernier, "Législation et pratiques relatives à la libre circulation des marchandises, personnes, services et capitaux au Canada" (1980), 3 *Revue d'intégration européenne* 267 at pp. 278–80.

136. R.S.C. 1970, c. I-15.

137. R.S.C. 1970, c. I-16.

138. R.S.C. 1970, c. I-17.

139. Arnett, *supra*, n. 88, p. 225; Bernier, *supra*, n. 2, p. 221; Hogg, *supra*, n. 29, pp. 301 and 302.

140. See Marvin G. Baer, "Harmonization of Canadian Insurance Law," in *Harmonization of Business Law in Canada*, volume 56 of the studies prepared for the Royal Commission on the Economic Union and Development Prospects for Canada (Toronto: University of Toronto Press, 1985).

141. Federally incorporated insurance companies make up 90 percent of the life insurance industry (see Canadian Life and Health Insurance Association, "The Vital Link: Financial Security and Capital Formation," brief no. 737 presented to the Royal Commission on the Economic Union and Development Prospects for Canada, Ottawa, October 1983, p. 33.

142. [1932] A.C. 318, p. 326. The provinces have been regulating securities for more than seventy years (see the historical aspects of securities regulation in Anisman and Hogg, *supra*, n. 48, p. 144; and Canada, Royal Commission of Inquiry on Dominion-Provincial Relations, *Report*, vol. 2, (Ottawa: Queen's Printer, 1940), pp. 59–62. See, generally, Chevrette and Marx, *supra*, n. 35, pp. 527 and 528.

143. *Duplain v. Cameron*, [1961] S.C.R. 693 (the requirement that anyone who issues promissory notes be registered is not incompatible with the provisions of the Federal act with respect to bills of exchange);

*Smith v. R.*, [1960] S.C.R. 776 (the Ontario act which regulates the trading of securities and sanctions false representations contained in a stock prospectus is not incompatible with the provisions of the Criminal Code with respect to the publication and the distribution of false prospectuses); *Malczenski v. Sansai Securities Ltd.*, [1975] 49 D.L.R. (3d) 629 (B.C.S.C.) (the obligation to deposit funds in trust for the benefit of clients, in the event of the bankruptcy of the depositor, is not incompatible with the federal *Bankruptcy Act*);

*Multiple Access Ltd. v. McCutcheon*, [1982] 2 S.C.R. 161; [1982] 44 N.R. 181 (the provisions of the Ontario *Securities Act* relating to insider trading are not incompatible with those of the federal act with respect to commercial companies).

144. Anisman and Hogg, *supra*, n. 48, p. 145, cited with approval by Mr. Justice Dickson in *Multiple Access Ltd. v. McCutcheon*, [1982] 44 N.R. 181, p. 203; [1982] 2 S.C.R. 161, p. 184.

145. *A.-G. Manitoba v. A.-G. Canada*, [1929] A.C. 260; Anisman and Hogg, *supra*, n. 48, pp. 151 and 152.

146. *Lymburn v. Mayland* [1932] A.C. 318; Hogg, *supra*, n. 29, c. 17, pp. 295 et seq.; Anisman and Hogg, *supra*, n. 48, pp. 143 et seq.

147. Ontario Securities Commission, "Report on the Implications for Canadian Capital Markets of the Provision by Financial Institutions of Access Discount Brokerage Services" (1983) 6 *Ontario Securities Commission Bulletin*, October 31, 1983, Special Supplement, p. 58 and, generally, pp. 57–66.

The Ontario Securities Commission has since specified the terms and conditions for registering discount brokers (Ontario Securities Commission, *Press Release — Greenline Investor/Discount Brokerage Services; Discount Brokerage Services — Provision by Financial Institutions of Access to Discount Brokerage Services*,(1984), 7 *Ontario Securities Commission Bulletin* January 27, 1984, pp. 453–61). The amendments passed require banks or trust companies which actively want to promote a discount brokerage service to register with the commission; the exemption applies only in a case in which the financial institution concerned does not actively promote or market the order execution access service" (ibid., p. 455). Amendments to the regulation have maintained the exemption of subscribers for certain types of brokerage operations, such as private investments by financial institutions which are authorized by their act of incorporation to carry out such transactions as of October 31, 1983. The Toronto-Dominion Bank's "Greenline Service" was approved by the Ontario Securities Commission (1984), 7 *Ontario Securities Commission Bulletin*, p. 670.

148. Ontario Securities Commission, *supra*, n. 147, pp. 48 and 49. It is interesting to note the Joint Securities Industry Committee's suggestions with respect to the intrinsic limits of the applicability of provincial regulations to banks:

> The Committee has received legal advice that because the regulation of banks and banking is a matter within federal jurisdiction, provincial legislative authorities cannot validly deny to the banks the right to carry on activities specifically permitted by the *Bank Act*. They may, of course, apply rates to the banks to regulate the conduct of those activities, but the rules may not have the indirect effect of precluding the banks from carrying on the activities. Since the *Bank Act* contains rates governing the extent to which banks may participate in securities activities, it is not possible for the provinces to exclude the banks from activities permitted by those rules (Joint Securities Industry Committee, Report, *Regulation and Ownership of Market Intermediaries in Canada*, September 1984, p. 26).

149. Quebec Securities Commission, "Avis divers: exercice de l'activité de courtier par les institutions financières" (1983), 14 *Québec Bulletin*, pp. 1.2.1 and 1.2.2 (May 27, 1983); and "Avis divers: rôle des institutions financières dans le Régime d'épargne-actions" (1983), 14 *Québec Bulletin*, p. 1.2.1 (November 25, 1983); *Instruction générale no Q-9. Courtiers, conseillers en valeurs et représentants*. The Quebec Securities Commission granted the Toronto-Dominion Bank limited registration as a stockbroker (Quebec Securities Commission, Decision 84-E-1420, November 23, 1984).

However, the National Bank was not treated in the same way when it launched an advertising campaign, in the fall of 1984, to encourage its clients to use its intermediary services to maintain, process, and execute securities orders (which were eligible under various tax benefit plans) without having obtained prior approval from the Quebec Securities Commission. The latter held that this amounted to "solicitation" under the act and that the bank's actions were therefore not exempt from registration as provided for in s. 154(1) of the *Securities Act* (R.S.Q., c. V.1, s. 154), and it ordered the bank to stop the campaign until such time as it obtained the required licence (see Quebec Securities Commission, *Banque nationale du Canada*, Decision no. 7220, December 4, 1984).

150. Philip Anisman, "Regulation of the Securities Market and Harmonization of Provincial Laws," in *Harmonization of Business Law in Canada*, volume 56 of the research studies prepared for the Royal Commission on the Economic Union and Development Prospects for Canada (Toronto: University of Toronto Press, 1985).

151. See Anisman and Hogg, *supra*, n. 48, pp. 145–50; Hogg, *supra*, n. 29, pp. 208–11; Anisman, *supra*, n. 150, pp. 61–71.

152. (1966) 56 D.L.R. (2d) 56 (Manitoba, C.A.) permission to appeal rejected sub. nom.; *West v. R.*, [1966] S.C.R. ix.

153. [1961] S.C.R. 584.

154. Anisman, *supra*, n. 150, p. 61–80; see the recent case, *Re Ontario Securities Commission and Electra Investments (Canada) Ltd.*, (1984) 45 O.R. (2d) 246. The problems related to the regulation of takeovers have recently been the subject of an in-depth

study by the Securities Industry Committee (*Report of the Securities Industry Com-mittee on Take-Over Bids — the Regulation of Take-Over Bids in Canada: Premium Private Agreement Transactions*, November, 1983). See also, by way of an example of attempts at harmonizing securities legislation, *An Act to Amend the Securities Act*, S.Q. 1984, c. 41.

155. *La Caisse populaire Notre-Dame Limitée v. Moyen*, [1967] 61 D.L.R. (2d) 118. See McDonald, *supra*, n. 18, p. 179.

156. *Cooperative Credit Associations Act*, R.S.C. 1970, c. C-29 [this act was passed in 1953 (S.C. 1953, c. 28)] and *Canadian Payments Association Act*, S.C. 1980–1981, c. 40.

157. See C.S. Axworthy, "Credit Unions in Canada: The Dilemma of Success" (1981), 31 *U.T.L.J.* 72, p. 91.

158. See Ontario, Ministry of Consumer and Commercial Relations, *supra*, n. 32, p. 1 and appendix; McDonald, *supra*, n. 18, pp. 164–66 and 179–82.

159. [1949] 1 D.L.R. 769, 57 Man. R. 66; [1949] 1 W.W.R. 323.

160. *The Agricultural Development Finance Act*, R.S.O. 1970, c. 11, s. 3, cited in McDonald, *supra*, n. 18, p. 183. The Ontario network included, as of September 1983, 21 branches with $684.8 million in public deposits ($728.9 million of combined public and government deposits) (Angela Barnes, "Competition Is Hurting Ontario Savings Offices," *Globe and Mail*, November 28, 1983, p. RB-15).

161. Treasury branches were established by Alberta during the economic crisis of the 1930s; they were to have been the heart of the new monetary system, which the Supreme Court invalidated in *Re Alberta Statutes*, [1938] S.C.R. 100. On March 31, 1983, the Alberta network included 130 branches as well as 103 agencies. From 1972 to 1983, the assets increased from $750 million to $2.99 billion, deposits increased from $287 million to $2.92 billion and loans from $150 million to $2.46 billion. Jane Becker, "Alberta's Treasury Branches Have $3.7 Million Loss," *Globe and Mail*, November 28, 1983, p. RB-15.

See also *Winnipeg Trustee v. Kenny*, [1924] 1 D.L.R. 952, p. 956. In this case, it was the Manitoba savings offices which were the object of the dispute. The Manitoba network disappeared in 1932 (McDonald, *supra*, n. 18, pp. 182 and 183). The constitu-tionality of the Treasury branches were also discussed in the *Breckenridge* case, but the majority of both the Alberta Court of Appeal and the Supreme Court did not feel that it was appropriate to deal with the issue in this type of case (*Breckenridge Speedway Ltd. v. Her Majesty The Queen in Right of Alberta* (1970) S.C.R. 175, pp. 184 et seq., Hall J. (dissenting); (1967) 64 D.L.R. (2d) 488, pp. 498 et seq. Porter J. (dissenting), and p. 511 et seq. Johnson J. (dissenting).

162. J.P. Williamson, "Recent Developments Affecting Mutual Funds," in Jacob S. Ziegel (ed.), *Studies in Canadian Company Law*, vol. 2 (Toronto: Butterworth, 1973), pp. 490–99.

See McDonald, *supra*, n. 18, pp. 172–74; and Canada, Committee on Mutual Funds and Investment Contracts, *Reports — Provincial and Federal Study* (Ottawa: Queen's Printer, 1969), pp. 17–22. Mutual Fund companies which are federally incor-porated are already supervised in part by federal business corporations legislation.

163. Canadian Association of Financial Corporations, "Submission to the Royal Commis-sion on the Economic Union and Development Prospects for Canada," Submission no. 862, section A-5.

164. *Investment Companies Act*, S.C. 1970–1971, 1972, c. 33, as amended; see E.A.A. Wighton and W.A. Smith, "Investment Companies Act" (1972), 100 *Canadian Char-tered Accountant*, June, p. 41.

165. *A.-G. Canada v. A.-G. Ontario*, [1937] A.C. 355.

166. Banting, *supra*, n. 127, pp. 191 and 192; Bruce Near, "Differing Legislation Creates Problem of Uniformity," *Globe and Mail*, August 24, 1984, p. R-6.

167. See Canada, House of Commons, Parliamentary Task Force on Pension Reform, *Report*, 1st session, 32nd Parliament, 1983, pp. 101–103.

As regards the positions of the provincial governments, see Alberta, *Proposals for Improving the Effectiveness of the Private Pension Plan System in Alberta*

(Edmonton, May 1, 1984); British Columbia, Ministry of Provincial Secretary and Government Services, *Developing a Pension Policy for the Future* (Victoria, June 1982); Manitoba, The Pension Commission of Manitoba, *Proposals for Amendments to the Pension Benefits Act* (Winnipeg, March 1983); Nova Scotia, Royal Commission on Pensions, *Report*, 2 vols. (Halifax, 1983); Ontario, Ministry of the Treasury and Economics, *Ontario Proposals for Pension Reform* (Toronto: Queen's Printer, 1984); Ontario, Royal Commission on the Status of Pensions in Ontario, *Report*, 10 vols. (Toronto: Queen's Printer, 1981); Quebec, *La sécurité financière des personnes âgées au Québec* (Rapport Cofirentes +) (Quebec: Éditeur officiel, March 1978).

168. See the case law cited in Hogg, *supra*, n. 29, pp. 317–19; Chevrette and Marx, *supra*, n. 35, pp. 608–10; *Tomell Investments Ltd. v. East Marstock Ltd.*, [1978] 1 S.C.R. 974; *Robinson v. Countrywide Factors Ltd.*, [1978] 1 S.C.R. 753; *Travelers Insurance Co. of Canada v. Corriveau*, [1982] 2 S.C.R. 866.

169. William A.W. Neilson, "Interjurisdictional Harmonization of Consumer Protection Laws and Administration in Canada" in *Perspectives on the Harmonization of Law in Canada*, volume 55 of the research studies prepared for the Royal Commission on the Economic Union and Development Prospects for Canada (Toronto: University of Toronto Press, 1985).

170. [1960] S.C.R. 571.

171. Neilson, supra, n. 169, pp. 16–24.

172. *Borrowers' and Depositors' Protection Act*, Bill C-16 (first reading, October 27, 1976), 2nd session, 32nd Parliament (Can.); Neilson, *supra*, n. 169, pp. 27–49.

173. *Act to Amend the Interest Act*, Bill C-36 (1st reading, May 25, 1984), 2nd session, 32nd Parliament (Can.).

174. Jordan, *supra*, n. 39, pp. 41 and 42. See, generally, Goldstein, *supra*, n. 111, pp. 291–309.

175. [1969] S.C.R. 383.

176. [1976] 2 S.C.R. 349; [1976] 42 D.L.R. (3d) 603. The province can also establish more onerous fiscal regulations with respect to non-residents [*Re Minister of Revenue for Ontario and Hala*, (1977) 81 D.L.R. (3d) 710]. It can be argued that controls over ownership similar to those deemed valid in the *Morgan* case might now be dismissed as being contrary to the guarantees with regard to mobility rights as set forth in s. 6 of the *Canadian Charter of Rights and Freedoms* (Schmeiser and Young, *supra*, n. 11, pp. 201 and 202). However, in light of the arguments upheld by the Supreme Court in the case of *Skapinker v. Law Society of Upper Canada* [(1983) 53 N.R. 169], this interpretation is not very convincing. On provincial controls over foreign investment, see, generally, H. Brun, "Le Québec peut empêcher la vente du sol québécois à des non-Québécois" (1975), 16 *Cahiers de droit* 973; Chevrette and Marx, *supra*, n. 35, pp. 1526–28. See also the amendment to the *Citizenship Act*, S.C. 1974–1975–1976, c. 108, s. 33.

177. *The Constitution Acts, 1867 to 1982*, ss. 92(2) and 92A. A summary of the negotiations that preceded the enactment of s. 92A is found in Alastair Lucas and Ian McDougall, "Petroleum and Natural Gas and Constitutional Change" in S.M. Beck and I. Bernier (eds.), *Canada and the New Constitution — The Unfinished Agenda* (Montreal: Institute for Research on Public Policy, 1983, pp. 32–35). See, generally on the provinces' powers of taxation, G.V. La Forest, *The Allocation of Taxing Power Under the Canadian Constitution*, 2nd ed. (Toronto: Canadian Tax Foundation, 1981); Anthony F. Sheppard, "Taxation Policy and the Canadian Economic Union," in *Fiscal Federalism*, volume 65 of the research studies prepared for the Royal Commission on the Economic Union and Development Prospects for Canada (Toronto: University of Toronto Press, 1985).

178. Hogg, *supra*, n. 29, p. 401. *A.-G. Alberta v. A.-G. Canada* (the taxation of banks case), [1939] A.C. 117, p. 128. See also, *A.-G. British Columbia v. MacDonald Murphy Lumber Co.* [1930] A.C. 357; *Texada Mines v. A.-G. British Columbia*, [1960] S.C.R. 713; *Canadian Industrial Gas and Oil Ltd. v. Government of Saskatchewan*, [1978] 2.
    The recent attempt by the Quebec Government to increase the rate of tax on the paid-up capital of banks was of doubtful validity, since it seems to have been designed

to punish the banks, the majority of which would have refused to participate in the provincial *Corvée-habitation* program (see the testimony of R. MacIntosh, president of the Canadian Banker's Association, *Transcripts* of the Royal Commission on the Economic Union and Development Prospects for Canada, volume 56, p. 11885) (Toronto, December 2, 1983).

179. Canada, Special Committee on Federal-Provincial Fiscal Arrangements, *Report* (Ottawa: Minister of Supply and Services Canada, 1981), p. 183.

180. Canada, Royal Commission on Dominion-Provincial Relations, *Report*, vol. 2 (Ottawa: Queen's Printer, 1940), pp. 113 and 134.

181. A historical summary of tax collection agreements in Canada is found in Canada, Special Committee on Federal-Provincial Fiscal Arrangements, *supra*, n. 179, p. 195–98. With respect to the special situation in Quebec, see Claude Forget, "Quebec's Experience with the Personal Income Tax," in Douglas G. Hartle et al. *A Separate Personal Income Tax for Ontario: An Economic Analysis* (Toronto: Ontario Economic Council, 1983), pp. 157–78. There is a discussion of the ins and outs of the debate with respect to tax harmonization in Richard M. Bird, "Tax Harmonization and Federal Finance: A Perspective on Recent Canadian Discussions" (1984), 10 *Canadian Public Policy* 253. See also Chevrette and Marx, *supra*, n. 35, pp. 1076–80.

182. Frank S. Miller, "Fiscal Federalism in Canada: The Record to Date, the Challenge Ahead," budget document in Ontario Budget 1982 (Toronto: Ministry of Treasury and Economics, 1982); Alberta, Government of Alberta White Paper, *Proposals for an Industrial and Science Strategy for Albertans 1985 to 1990* (Edmonton, July 1984), pp. 62 and 63; Hugh McCurtis, *British Columbia Budget* (Victoria, March 1981), p. 31.

183. See Ontario Economic Council, *A Separate Personal Income Tax for Ontario*, an Ontario Economic Council Position Paper (Toronto: The Council, 1983), pp. 20–28. See also D.G. Hartle et al., *A Separate Personal Income Tax for Ontario: An Economic Analysis* (Toronto: Ontario Economic Council, 1983).

184. Ontario Economic Council, *supra*, no. 183, ibid., p. 25. The federal government has also refused to administer the tax credits proposed by Alberta and Saskatchewan (ibid., pp. 25 and 26).

185. Allan J. MacEachen, *Federal-Provincial Fiscal Arrangements in the Eighties*, submission to the Special Committee on Federal-Provincial Fiscal Arrangements, April 23, 1981, p. 54, cited in *supra*, n. 179, p. 183.

186. Martin Martin, Service des études, Quebec Securities Commission. "Le Régime d'épargne-sections du Québec — un programme unique en Amérique, document presented at the Ninth Conference of the International Organization of Securities Commissions and similar organizations held in Toronto from July 29 to August 3, 1984; "Les ventes d'actions admissibles au REA ont doublé en 1983," *Les Affaires* (Montreal), January 21, 1984, p. 4.

187. Thomas J. Courchene, "Analytical Perspectives on the Canadian Economic Union" in Trebilcock et al. (eds.), *Federalism and the Canadian Union* (Toronto: University of Toronto Press for the Ontario Economic Council, 1983), p. 55.

188. Alberta, *supra*, n. 182, pp. 62 and 63.

189. Sheppard, *supra*, n. 177.

190. Canada, *supra*, n. 17, p. 2.

191. Hogg, *supra*, n. 29, pp. 349–51.

192. S.Q. 1978, c. 86, as amended by S.W. 1982, c. 52, ss. 48 and 49; R.S.Q., C.A. 31, para. 1(d), see ss. 1(b), 2, 3, and 8.

193. *An Act Respecting Crown Trust Company*, S.O. 1983, c. 7. The Ontario legislature also passed, in December 1982, some amendments to the *Loan and Trust Corporations Act* which, inter alia, gave the registrar the power to seize the assets of a trust company subject to the act: (*Loan and Trust Corporations Amendment Act*, S.O. 1982, c. 62, s. 3).

194. See Bernier, *supra*, n. 135.

195. Canada, Senate, Standing Committee on Legal and Constitutional Affairs, *Proceed-*

*ings on the Subject-Matter of Bill S-31* (Act to Limit Shareholding in Certain Corporations), December 16, 1982, p. 5201. See Hogg, *supra*, n. 29, pp. 363 and 364.

196. *Supra*, n. 180, pp. 56 and 57.

197. *Canada Business Corporations Act*, S.C. 1974–76, c. 33. See Jacob S. Ziegel, "Harmonization of Provincial Laws, with Particular Reference to Commercial, Consumer and Corporate Law," in *Harmonization of Business Law In Canada*, volume 56 of the research studies prepared for the Royal Commission on the Economic Union and Development Prospects for Canada, Ottawa, Ministry of Supply and Services Canada (Toronto: University of Toronto Press, 1985).

198. [1936] S.C.R. 427, p. 434. See also the recent decision of the Saskatchewan Court of Queen's Bench in *Dunbar v. A.-G. Saskatchewan* (1984) 33 Sask R. 193. On preferential buying policies, see the interesting analysis of the Quebec policy in this regard by Ivan Bernier, "L'économie québécoise face à la concurrence extérieure : les fondements scientifiques de la politique d'achat préférentiel du Québec" (1984), 15 *Études internationales* 61; Tupper, *supra*, n. 117, p. 25 et seq.; Economic Council of Canada, *supra*, n. 35, p. 1047; Driedger, *supra*, n. 117, pp. 132 and 133.

199. *Constitution Act, 1867*, 30–31 Victoria, c. 3 (U.K.), s. 92(3), Canada, *supra*, n. 180, pp. 82, 83 and 122–124.

200. Jacques Parizeau, Verbatim Transcript, Federal-provincial First Ministers' Conference on the Constitution, Ottawa, September 8 to 13, 1980 (Ottawa: Canadian Intergovernmental Conference Secretariat, Document Centre, 1980), p. 789.

201. Canada, Royal Commission on Banking and Finance, *Report* (Ottawa: Queen's Printer, 1964), p. 378 (hereafter the Porter Report).

202. Ibid., p. 379. With respect to government institutions, the Porter Commission should have added that any measure which encouraged excessive expansion of these institutions "might raise an issue for the federal authorities and lead to subsequent review of this recommendation" (ibid., p. 378). The argument that depositors must be protected as justification for the extension of banking legislation to all banking institutions has lost its force since the creation of the Canada Deposit Insurance Corporation, which controls financial institutions on behalf of the federal government and in a manner which the Economic Council of Canada considers appropriate. See Economic Council of Canada, Efficiency and Regulation: A Study of Deposit Institutions (Ottawa: Minister of Supply and Services Canada, 1976), p. 80 and 81.

203. Porter Report, *supra*, n. 201, p. 375, see pp. 563 and 564.

204. François-Albert Angers, *Mémoire au Comité des institutions financières: la Banque du Canada et le contrôle des institutions financières*, vol. 1, p. 54. The economist Angers has severely criticized the ideas of the Porter Commission (ibid., pp. 40, 76–84) with respect to its recommendation that provincial deposit institutions should be subject to banking legislation on the grounds of efficiency (surveillance and inspection), logic and equity (similar institutions must receive similar treatment) as well as healthy competition (Porter Report, *supra*, n. 201, pp. 559–67).

205. Porter Report, *supra*, n. 201, p. 393. See also pp. 390–92. With respect to the federal government's requirement that all deposit institutions must have cash reserves, see, generally, John F. Chant and James W. Dean, "An Approach to the Regulation of Banking Institutions in a Federal State" (1982), 20 *Osgoode Hall L. J.* 721, p. 739 and 740.

206. Porter Report, *supra*, n. 201, p. 393.

207. Quebec, Comité d'étude sur les institutions financières, *supra*, n. 21, p. 214; see also pp. 181–214.

208. Gerald Bouey writes: "Would Canada's monetary policy have a greater impact if the other financial institutions which can take deposits were directly affected by the activities of the Bank of Canada as are the Chartered Banks?" (*Bank of Canada Review*, September 1974, p. 17).

209. The Canada Deposit Insurance Corporation and the Régie de l'assurance-dépôts du Québec came to an agreement on January 22, 1969, defining the context of their mutual relations. A historical summary of deposit insurance is found in E.P. Neufeld, *supra*, n. 21, pp. 439–41. On the creation of the Régie de l'assurance-dépôts du

Québec, see, generally, Quebec, Comité d'étude sur les institutions financières, *supra*, n. 21, pp. 129–46. On the nature of the agreements between the Canada Deposit Insurance Corporation and the Régie de l'assurance-dépôts, see Economic Council of Canada, *supra*, n. 202, p. 14.

210. Canada, Department of Finance, *supra*, n. 4, pp. 8 and 18–21. The federal government first tabled a bill (Bill C-57) with respect to the revision of banking legislation in May 1978. The bill (Bill C-15) was reintroduced in November 1978.

   In June 1979, the Progressive Conservative party came to power, and it was then, in October 1979, that Bill C-14 was tabled before the House of Commons. It will be noted that this version of the revision of banking legislation was significantly different from previous versions. Following the re-election of the Liberal Party of Canada in February 1980, the bill (then Bill C-6) was reintroduced, in May 1980, before the new Parliament (see, generally, J. Harvey Perry, "Bank Act Revision: Report from a Survivor" (1980), 87 *Canadian Banker and ICB Review* (4), pp. 60 et seq.

211. See the Fédération de Québec des caisses populaires Desjardins, the Fédération de Montréal des caisses Desjardins, the Fédération des caisses d'économie du Québec, the Ligue des caisses d'économie du Québec, the Fédération des caisses d'établissement du Québec, the Fédération des caisses d'entraide économique du Québec, *Mémoire à l'honorable Donald S. Macdonald, ministre des Finances du Canada, au sujet du livre blanc sur la révision de la législation bancaire canadienne, octobre 1976*.

   A summary of the debate (which set the banks against the caisses populaires and the federal government against the Quebec government) is given in François Moreau, *Le capital financier québécois* (Quebec: Éditions coopératives Albert Saint-Martin, Centrale de l'enseignement du Québec, 1981), pp. 117–24.

212. Chant and Dean, *supra*, n. 205, p. 739.

213. Economic Council of Canada, *supra*, n. 202, pp. 54, 60, 61, 71, 72, and 74–94.

214. Canada, Senate Standing Committee on Banking, Trade and Commerce, *Report of the Committee on the White Paper on Canadian Banking Legislation*, June 28, 1977, p. 44:31. See also pp. 44:18, 44:19, 44:30; see also Bouey, *supra*, n. 208, p. 23.

215. Canada, Senate, Standing Committee on Finance, Trade and Economic Affairs, Second Report to the House (concerning the subject matter of Bill C-15, 1978 act to revise banking legislation), March 19, 1979, p. 45:5.

216. See Robert M. MacIntosh, "An Eventful Year" (1981), 88 *Canadian Banker and ICB Review* (4), pp. 31–34. Parliament did, however, use a functionalist approach with regard to foreign banks by stipulating that those wanting to take deposits negotiable by cheque operate in conformity with federal banking legislation (see, *supra*, n. 36).

   It is also interesting to note that proposals for the revision of federal legislation applicable to federal trust and loan companies did not make provision for the obligatory deposit by such companies of cash reserves in the Bank of Canada. Thus, the federal government seems to favour giving these companies treatment similar to that given to provincial financial institutions; see Canada, Department of Insurance, *Summary and Guide to the Proposed Revision and Consolidation of the Trust Companies Act and the Loan Companies Act*, Ottawa, Department of Insurance, July 1982, p. 9 (hereafter "Summary and guide"). Thus, the banks are still the only financial institutions that have to maintain cash reserves. However, the prescribed levels of such reserves have been substantially reduced (see J.H. Perry, "Bank Act Revision Act" (1980), 87 *Canadian Banker and ICB Review* (6), pp. 4–8); *Banks and Banking Law Revision Act, 1980*, S.C. 1980–81, c. 40, s. 208; and *Regulation with Respect to Reserves*, DORS/81, May 28, 1981.

217. See William A. Dimma, "Remarks," Sixty-eighth Annual Meeting of the Investment Dealers Association of Canada, Jasper, Alta., June 18, 1984. Dimma was at that time the chairman of the Advisory Committee on Financial Institutions.

218. Robert Stephens, "Ontario to Investigate Financial Institutions," *Globe and Mail*, June 14, 1984, p. RD-1. The committee made its interim report public on January 30, 1985 (see Interim Report of the Ontario Task Force on Financial Institutions, December 1984).

219. Quebec, *Comité d'étude sur les institutions financières*, *supra*, n. 21, pp. 124 and 150.

220. Canada, Department of Finance, *The Regulation of Canadian Financial Institutions*, Executive Summary (Ottawa: Minister of Supply and Services Canada, 1985), pp. 11–29 (hereafter the "green paper"). See also the summary of the ins and outs of the current confusion in the financial markets presented by Pierre Lortie, Chairman of the Montreal Stock Exchange (*The Re-Regulation of Financial Institutions: The Morning After* (Quebec: Canadian Life and Health Insurance Association, annual meeting of the investment section, June 20, 1984, pp. 7–9); the enlightening suggestions of William A. Dimma, chairman of the federal Advisory Committee on Financial Institutions, *supra*, n. 217, pp. 5–21; and those of Mickey Cohen, "The Important Role and Future of the Financial Service Industry — A Domestic and International Context," in *Institutions in Transition: The Changing Nature of the Canadian Financial Services Industry* (Toronto: Strategic Planning Forum, 1983), pp. 3 et seq.

221. *Bank Act*, S.C. 1966–67, c. 87, s.10(4), 18(3), 33(1)(d) and 52–57; Neufeld, *supra*, n. 21, pp. 100 and 101; Canada, Department of Finance, *supra*, n. 4, pp. 27 and 28.

222. *Banks and Banking Law Revision Act, 1980*, S.C. 1980–81, c. 40, ss. 36(2), 110, 110.1 and 174(2)(e).

223. Ibid., ss. 110.1(4), 114(1)(2)(4) and (5). The provinces cannot, however, directly incorporate a bank by letters patent (ibid., s. 8a).
    A new bank is a Canadian bank incorporated after December 31, 1967 [ibid., s. 114(1)]; see also s. 257(1)(a)(iii) and (2)(d).

224. Ibid., s. 114(3)(4)(5). Canada, Department of Finance, *supra*, n. 4, p. 22. A financial corporation is a Canadian financial institution which does not accept deposits [s. 109(1)].

225. Ibid., ss. 111(6) and 2(1) and 109(2).

226. Ibid., ss. 173 to 214; *Central Computer Services Ltd. v. Toronto Dominion Bank* (1979), 95 D.L.R. (3d) 278.

227. *Banks and Banking Law Revision Act, 1980*, S.C. 1980–81, c. 40, ss. 109(1), 173, 174(2)(a),(b), 174(3),(4) and (19), 190 and 191.

228. The entry of banks into the field of consumer credit ought to alter considerably the activities of financial corporations, since over 80 percent of their activities are now in the commercial sector (see Association of Canadian Financial Corporations, *supra*, n. 163, point B, and the testimony of the Canadian Association of Financial Corporations, *Transcripts* of the Royal Commission on the Economic Union and Development Prospects for Canada, vol. 57, Toronto, December 2, 1983, pp. 120–40).

229. Thomas J. Courchene, *Economic Management and the Division of Powers*, vol. 67 of the research studies prepared for the Royal Commission on the Economic Union and Development Prospects for Canada (Toronto: University of Toronto Press, 1985). However, the banks must respect the 10 percent ceiling for liability-deposits payable in Canadian currency and bank debentures issued and outstanding in Canadian currency; *Banks and Banking Law Revision Act, 1980*, S.C. 1980–81, c. 40, s. 176.

230. *Banks and Banking Law Revision Act, 1980*, S.C. 1980–81, c. 40, ss. 173(1)(i), (j), (m), (n), (o), (4), (5), 174(a), (j), 191, 192, 193(2),(3),(6) and (7).

231. Quebec, Ministry of Finance, *supra*, n. 4, p. 35; Canada, Senate Standing Committee on Banking, Trade and Commerce, *supra*, n. 214, pp. 44–68.

232. *Banks and Banking Law Revision Act, 1980*, S.C. 1980–81, c. 40, ss. 173(1)(c), (h), 190 to 192; see Ontario Securities Commission, *supra*, n. 147, p. 41; Canada, Senate, Standing Committee on Banking, Trade and Commerce, *Report* of the Committee (on Bill C-15, 1978 bill to revise banking legislation), March 7, 1979, pp. 30:120 and 30:121. See, generally, Ian F.G. Baxter, *The Law of Banking*, 3d ed. (Toronto: Carswell, 1981), pp. 34–36.
    On the state of the power of banks with respect to securities before the enactment of the *Banks and Banking Law Revision Act, 1980*, see J. Peter Williamson, "Canadian Financial Institutions" in Canada, Department of Consumer and Corporate Affairs, *Proposals for a Securities Market Law for Canada*, vol. 3, *Background Papers* (Ottawa: Minister of Supply and Services Canada, 1979), pp. 862–911.

233. Ontario Securities Commission, *Report on the Implications*, *supra*, n. 147, p. 40.

234. Ibid., pp. 26–29, 41, 42 and 48–52. With regard to the abolition of fixed brokerage

fees, see R.L. Beck and G.B. Reschenthaler, "Ending Securities Commission Fee Regulation: Rationale and Economic Effects" (1982–83), 7 *Can. Bus. L. J.* 377. Quebec also opted for the introduction of discount brokerage (Quebec Securities Commission, *Decision 6696*, June 25, 1982).

Some are afraid that, through discount brokerage, the banks will eventually undermine the viability of institutions working specifically in the negotiation and canvassing of securities, and that they will ultimately absorb them into their own institutional networks (Ontario Securities Commission, *Report on the Implications*, *supra*, n. 147, pp. 47–52). See also, "Banks and Broking: Prospects Uncertain," *Financial Post* (Toronto), November 12, 1983, p. S-2. William D. Moull, "Constitutional Aspects of Bank Regulation — Silence on the Green Line" (1985), 10 *Can. Bus. L. J.* 71.

235. *Banks and Banking Law Revision Act*, 1980, S.C. 1980–81, c. 40, ss. 193(1),(1)(ii), (2), (6), (12), (13), (14), and 194.

236. Ibid., s. 174(2)(h), (13), (14) and 193(1) "bank service corporation," (5)(a), (2)(6) and (6).

237. See *Banks and Banking Law Revision Act, 1980*, S.C. 1980–81, c. 40, ss. 2, 5, 6, 8(d), 28, 110, 110.1, 115, 155, 156, 159, 302, 303, 304, 305, 307 and 310. A representative office represents a foreign bank and must not be occupied or controlled by a company incorporated under Canadian legislation or under provincial legislation [*Banks and Banking Law Revision Act, 1980, S.C. 1980–81*, c. 40, s. 302(3)]. See the list of representative offices in the *Globe and Mail*, April 6, 1984, p. R-2. It should be noted that foreign banks were previously interfered with on Canadian financial markets because of provincial regulation (see Bouey, *supra*, n. 208, pp. 21 and 22). Finally, it should be pointed out that Schedule B of the *Bank Act* includes not only subsidiaries of foreign banks but more generally any bank of which a single shareholder (along with associates) owns more than 10 percent of the shares of the latter. Thus, there is at least one "Canadian" (as opposed to "foreign") bank in Schedule B, for example the Morguard Bank of Canada.

238. Ibid., s. 302(1)(a), (b) and (8)(d).

239. Ibid., ss. 302 and 305.

240. Ibid., s. 22(5), 36(2), 46(2), 110, 114, 173, 174 and 200.

241. A subsidiary of a foreign bank can be established only if the Minister of Finance of Canada feels that that bank "is likely to stimulate competition in Canada" and only if the country of origin of the foreign banks which are shareholders of the subsidiary of the foreign bank "allow or will allow similarly advantageous conditions" to Canadian banks [ibid., s. 8(d)]. Angela Barnes, "U.S. Study May Have Spurred Bank Bill," *Globe and Mail*, April 14, 1984, p. B-1; see also Martin Mittelstaedt, "Bank Proposals Called 'Betrayal'," *Globe and Mail*, April 20, 1984, p. B-3; Canada, House of Commons, Standing Committee on Finance, Trade and Economic Affairs, *Proceedings and Evidence*, October 27, 1983, p. 5.

242. *Act to Amend the Bank Act*, S.C. 1984, c. 30.

243. S.C. 1964–65, c. 40, s. 30; see R.S.C. 1970, c. T-16, as amended by R.S.C. 1970, 1st suppl. c. 47, ss. 37 to 41.

244. S.C. 1964–65, c. 40, s. 38; see R.S.C. 1970, c. L-12, as amended by R.S.C. 1970, 1st suppl. c. 24, ss. 44 to 48.

245. *Trust Companies Act*, R.S.C. 1970, c. T-16, s. 19, as amended; *Loan Companies Act*, R.S.C. 1970, c. L-12, s. 19, as amended.

246. Manitoba: *The Corporations Act*, S.M. 1976, c. 40, s. 100, pp. 343–48.

Alberta: *Trust Companies Act*, R.S.A. 1980, c. T-9, ss. 66–69. Three-quarters of the members of the board of directors of a trust company incorporated in Alberta must be Canadian citizens and must reside in Canada (ibid., s. 29).

Ontario: *Loan and Trust Corporations Act*, R.S.O. 1980, c. 249, ss. 77 to 80, as amended. A majority of the directors of a loan or trust company incorporated in Ontario must be Canadian citizens and must usually reside in Canada (ibid., s. 57).

247. Nova Scotia: *Trust Companies Act*, R.S.N.S. 1967, c. 316, s. 17. A majority of the members of the board of directors of a trust company incorporated under the laws of this province must be residents of Nova Scotia.

Quebec: *Loi sur les compagnies de fidéicommis*, R.S.Q. 1977, c. C-41. Trust companies which are not incorporated under Quebec legislation must be registered pursuant to the conditions fixed by the government (see Tetley Report, *supra*, n. 132, p. 158).

Saskatchewan: *Trust Companies Act*, R.S.S. 1978, c. T-21, s. 19. A majority of the members of the board of directors of a trust company must be residents of Saskatchewan and British subjects. As regards trust companies not incorporated under the laws of Saskatchewan, see *The Trust and Loan Companies Act*, R.S.S. 1978, c. T-22, s. 7.

British Columbia: *Trust Companies Act*, R.S.B.C. 1979, c. 412, s. 21. A majority of the members of the board of directors of a trust company must be residents of British Columbia and subjects of Her Majesty; *Companies Act*, R.S.B.C. 1979, c. 59, s. 133 (by the terms of this act, a majority of the members of the board of directors of a company incorporated under this act must be normally resident in Canada, and one of the members of the board of directors of any company must be normally resident in the province.

Newfoundland: *Trust and Loan Companies (Licensing) Act*, S.N.F. 1974, c. 120. The minister responsible for the application of the act may, with the approval of the Lieutenant-Governor in Council, remove the requirements of certain sections and completely exempt a company which is in effect controlled by residents of the province.

248. Canada, Department of Insurance, *supra*, n. 31, pp. 11 and 12.

249. S.Q. 1978, c. 86, as amended.

250. *An Act to Amend the Loan and Trust Corporations Act*, S.O. 1982, c. 62.

251. Canada, Department of Insurance, *supra*, n. 31, pp. 12–16. The Liberal government considered the practicalities of imposing a standard of 10 percent only if the provinces harmonized their legislation in this regard (ibid., p. 13). It should be noted that the federal government is also considering, again according to the model of the *Bank Act*, allowing foreign trust companies to do business in Canada (ibid., pp. 9 and 10); for the position of the Progressive Conservative government, see green paper, *supra*, n. 220, pp. 5, 37–40.

252. Ontario, Ministry of Consumer and Commercial Relations, *supra*, n. 32, pp. 22–25.

253. Canada, Department of Insurance, *supra*, n. 31, pp. 19 and 20; Ontario, Ministry of Consumer and Commercial Relations, *supra*, n. 32, p. 30.

254. Canada, Department of Insurance, *supra*, n. 31, p. 20. Canada, Department of Insurance, *supra*, n. 216, p. 1; *Proposed Revision and Consolidation of the Trust Companies Act and the Loan Companies Act* [s. 186(5)(6) hereafter "Proposed Revision"]; green paper, *supra*, n. 228, pp. 46 and 47.

   By the end of 1981, there were 33 federally chartered companies (assets of $20 billion) and 16 provincially chartered companies (assets of $5 billion) and 32 federally chartered trust companies (with deposits of $22 billion), as well as 67 provincially chartered trust companies (with deposits of $16 billion).

255. Fiducie du Québec: Quebec Securities Commission, *Decision 83-E-1661*, October 6, 1983, revised by *Decision 83-E-2038*, November 29, 1983, and by *Decision 84-E-896*, May 8, 1984, which were collectively repealed and replaced by *Decision 84-E-1176*, September 6, 1984.

   Royal Trust: Quebec Securities Commission, *Decision 83-E-1979*, November 18, 1983, revised by *Decision 84-E-895*, May 8, 1984, which were collectively repealed and replaced by *Decision 84-E-1179*, September 12, 1984.

256. National Trust: Quebec Securities Commission, *Decision 84-E-180*, January 20, 1984, repealed and replaced by *Decision 84-E-1181*, September 12, 1984.

   General Trust of Canada: Quebec Securities Commission, *Decision 84-E-77*, March 30, 1984, repealed and replaced by *Decision 84-E-1180*.

   Canada Trust Company: Quebec Securities Commission, *Decision 84-E-1374*, November 27, 1984.

257. Ontario, Ministry of Consumer and Commercial Relations, *supra*, n. 32, pp. 19, 20, 29 and 30.

258. *Canadian and British Insurance Companies Act*, R.S.C. 1970, c. I-15, ss. 18 and 19; see also s. 20.

259. *Foreign Insurance Companies Act*, R.S.C. 1970, c. I-16, s. 12.

260. *Companies Act*, R.S.B.C. 1979, c. 59, s. 133; *Business Corporations Act*, R.S.S. 1978, c. B-10, ss. 100 and 109; *Alberta Insurance Act*, R.S.A. 1980, c. I-5, s. 138.

261. *Insurance Act*, R.S.B.C. 1979, c. 200, s. 120; *An Act Respecting Insurance and Insurers*, R.S.M. 1970, c. I-40, s. 397 et seq.

262. *An Act Respecting Insurance*, R.S.Q. c. A-32, ss. 43 to 50 and 91, as amended by the *Act to Amend the Act Respecting Insurance*, S.Q. 1984, c. 22, s. 15 to 21 and 33.

263. See the examples of the Traders Group Limited, Trilon Financial Corporation and Power Corporation (Canadian Banker's Association. *The Regulation of Financial Institutions in Canada*: submission no. 696 to the Royal Commission on the Economic Union and Development Prospects for Canada, Table 2, p. 19; Eric Starkman, "Power Corp. Assembles a New Financial Firm in the Banks and Caisse," *The Gazette* (Montreal), April 12, 1984.

264. Canadian Life and Health Insurance Association, *Financial Services for the Future — Submission*, submission to the Royal Commission on the Economic Union and Development Prospects for Canada, Toronto, September 1983, pp. 12, 20, 23 and 62. The association's submission contains an impressive number of suggestions based on a significant increase in the power of companies. See the summary of the demands of the association in Canadian Life and Health Insurance Association, *Financial Services for the Future — Highlights*, Toronto, September 1983, p. 19.

265. S.Q. 1984, c. 22. See Canadian Banker's Association, *Observations on Bill 75 — Act to Amend the Act Respecting Insurance and Other Legislative Provisions*, June 1984; Dimma, *supra*, n. 217, p. 2; on the American situation, see Arthur Anderson & Co., Roma, *Changing Horizons for Insurance: Charting a Course for Success*, 1984, s. 1.

266. Ibid., s. 10, adding ss. 33(1), 33(2) and 33(3) to *An Act Respecting Insurance*, R.S.Q., c. A-32; Quebec Securities Commission, "Avis : projet de modification de l'instruction générale no. Q-9" (1984), 15 *Québec Bulletin*, no. 20 (May); "Avis d'audience publique: le cumul d'activités en valeurs mobilières et en assurances" (1984), 15 *Québec Bulletin*, no. 35, August 31, p. 1.1.1. See the following submissions to the Quebec Securities Commission: The Laurentian Group Corporation, *Cumul des activités des intermédiaires — rapport soumis à la Commission des valeurs mobilières du Québec*, July 31, 1984; Canadian Life and Health Insurance Association, *Cumul d'activités*, July 13, 1984; Investment Funds Institute of Canada, *Dual Registration in Securities and Insurance*, July 16, 1984; Daniel Côté and Yves Loranger, Service de l'inscription, Direction de l'encadrement des marchés, Quebec Securities Commission, *Le cumul d'activités — Sommaire des mémoires présentés devant la Commission*, September 24, 1984. See, generally, Jean-Marie Bouchard, inspector general of financial institutions in Quebec, "La réforme québécoise des institutions financières au Québec" (1985), 53 *Assurances* 7.

267. *Act to Amend the Act Respecting Insurance*, S.Q. 984, c. 22, s. 10, adding ss. 33(2) and 33(3) to the *Act Respecting Insurance*, R.S.Q., c. A-32; *Act Respecting Insurance*, R.S.Q., c. A-32, ss. 206 and 245–47, as amended by S.Q. 1984, c. 22, ss. 43 and 48.

268. See Canadian Banker's Association, *Comments on the Competitive Position of the Securities Industry in Domestic and International Financial Markets*, November 1984, pp. 5, 6 and appendix A (from 1976 to 1983 "free credit balances" went from some $102 million to more than $1,170 million); Dennis Slocum, "Midland Doherty Plans Cheque Service," *Globe and Mail*, June 19, 1984, p. RB-1.

269. *Securities Act*, R.S.O. 1980, c. 466, ss. 132–136. See *Report of the Committee to Study the Requirements and Sources of Capital and the Implications on Non-Residents for the Canadian Securities Industry* (Moore Report), May 1970; Williamson, *supra*, n. 232, pp. 793 et seq. Ontario Securities Commission, *Report of the Securities Ownership Committee*, Toronto, April 1972, pp. 1, 97–117 and 121–26; Donaldson, *supra*, n. 53, p. 564. It will be noted that the standards set have respected the vested interests of foreign investors with investments above the ceilings of 10 percent and 25 percent in Canadian brokerage firms such as Merrill Lynch Canada Inc. and Bache Securities Inc.

For a review of the 1984 status of securities firms which benefited from this protection, see Ontario Securities Commission, *A Regulatory Framework for Entry into and Ownership of the Ontario Securities Industry*, February 1985, pp. 4, 5 and appendix I (hereafter, 1985 OSC Report). However, the effectiveness of these controls was only relative, since they did not apply to brokerage firms exempted from the requirement to register with the Ontario Securities Commission; see Ontario Securities Commission, "Report to the Minister of Consumer and Commercial Relations on the Application of Ontario Securities Legislation to Non-Resident Securities Firms not Currently Registered in Ontario" (1979), *Ontario Securities Commission Bulletin* 420 (December).

270. *General Regulations of the Toronto Stock Exchange*, parts V and VI; Investment Dealers Association of Canada, *Act of Incorporation, Statutes and Regulations*, July 1984, Statutes, title 1, s. 1(iaa), title V, ss. 7 and 10.

271. Quebec, Comité d'étude sur les institutions financières, *supra*, n. 21, pp. 238, 239 and 263 (Parizeau Report); Quebec, Ministère des Institutions financières, Compagnies et Coopératives, *Études sur l'industrie des valeurs mobilières au Québec — rapport final* (Quebec, June 1972), vol. 1, pp. 141–47 (Bouchard Report); Tetley Report, *supra*, n. 132, pp. 155–58.

272. "Re Reynolds Securities (Canada) Ltd" (1978), 9 *Québec Bulletin* 1; Quebec Securities Commission, Instruction générale no. Q-9, s. 9(5); see Anisman, *supra*, n. 150; Tetley Report, *supra*, n. 132, p. 157, *Règlements et règles de la Bourse de Montréal*, regulation III and rule IX (see order of the Quebec Securities Commission with respect to the Montreal Stock Exchange on this subject (Quebec Securities Commission, "La propriété et la diversification des maisons de courtage," decision 6861 (1983), 14 *Québec Bulletin* no. 24 (June 15, 1981), p. 2.1.20 and 2.1.21). The commission recently repeated its position of principle to the effect that it was not opposed to the entry of foreign firms: see "L'appel public à l'épargne par les courtiers, Decision 6451" (1981), 12 *Québec Bulletin* no. 32 (August 13, 1981); and Decision 6861, June 15, 1983. The Quebec Securities Commission has, moreover, confirmed that it was not appropriate to review its Decision 6451 of August 13, 1981.

273. Ontario Securities Commission, *Policy No. 4.1: Public Ownership of Dealers, Conditions of Registration and Institutional Ownership*, ss. 2 and 4; Investment Dealers Association of Canada, *Articles of Incorporation*, July 1984, title I, s. 1(eg), (ega), (ka) and title V, ss. 1, 5, 8 et seq.; *General Regulations of the Toronto Stock Exchange*, relevant definitions in part I. It should be pointed out that the Ontario legislation is silent with respect to the ownership of brokerage firms by investors other than commercial investors (including financial institutions). See also, Ontario Securities Commission, *supra*, n. 269, pp. 95, 96 and 188–92; *Report of the Joint Industry Committee on Public Ownership in the Canadian Securities Industry*, March 1981; 1985 OSC Report, *supra*, n. 269, appendix 8.

274. *Report of the Joint Industry Committee on Guidelines for Diversification of the Securities Industry*, September 23, 1976, cited in Williamson, *supra*, n. 232, pp. 785 and 786; see the existing measures, Toronto Stock Exchange, *General By-Law*, part VII, p. 275.

275. Ontario Securities Commission, *supra*, n. 273, part C; see Ontario Securities Commission, "Report to the Minister of Consumer and Commercial Relations Regarding: (I) Institutional Ownership of Securities Dealers Registered Under the Securities Act and (II) Diversification into other Businesses by Securities Dealers Registered Under the Securities Act" (1982), 5 *Ontario Securities Commission Bulletin* 23 (December 31), pp. 597A, 598A and 605A–608A; and Ontario Securities Commission, "Report on the Implications for Canadian Capital Markets of the Provision by Financial Institutions of Access Discount Brokerage Services" (1983), 6 *Ontario Securities Commission Bulletin* (October 31) "special supplement", pp. 75 and 76.

In addition, policy statement 4.1 clearly affirms that "except with the consent of the Commission and, where the dealer is a member of the TSE, the IDA or both, no dealer shall, directly or indirectly, engage in business as a bank, a loan or a trust company or an insurance company" (ibid., s. 3). The commission resolved not to grant permission pursuant to this section (ibid., point C).

276. The Ontario Securities Commission reopened the debate on the participation of

foreign and Canadian investors in the ownership of brokerage firms. See Ontario Securities Commission, "Policy Review: Competition Position of the Securities Industry in Domestic and International Financial Markets (1984), 7 *Ontario Securities Commission Bulletin* (May 4), p. 1907; and "Securities Industry Policy Review: Preliminary Issues Paper" (1984), 7 *Ontario Securities Commission Bulletin* (June 29), p. 2766. The hearings were held in November and December 1984. Very divergent points of view were presented. Thus, the joint committee of the securities industry did not hesitate to recommend maintaining existing controls over foreign investment, over non-commercial investors, over flexibility in the field of networking, and over the clear distinction between financial intermediaries and market intermediaries; and the adoption of the regulatory framework to ensure the separation of functions between the international and Canadian capital markets (*Report of the Joint Industry Committee, Regulation and Ownership of Market Intermediaries in Canada*, September 19, 1984); Ontario Securities Commission, "Securities Industry Review — Request for Comments in Response to the Report of the Joint Securities Industry Committee" (1984), 7 *Ontario Securities Commission Bulletin*, pp. 3985 et seq.). See also, among others, the submission of the Canadian Banker's Association, *Comments on the Competitive Position of the Securities Industry in Domestic and International Financial Markets* (Ottawa, November 1984); Royal Bank of Canada, *Submission to the Ontario Securities Commission — The Adequacy and Relevance of Regulations Governing the Ownership and Registration of Securities Firms*, November 29, 1984; Orion Royal Bank Limited, *Ontario Securities Commission Policy Review, Competitive Position on the Securities Industry in Domestic and International Financial Markets*, November 29, 1984; Thomas J. Courchene, *A Really Secure Industry or a Real Securities Industry — A Submission to the Ontario Securities Commission in Respect of Its Securities Industry Review*, November 28, 1984. For a complete list of submissions received by the Ontario Securities Commission, see 1985 OSC Report, *supra*, n. 269, appendix 6.

277. 1985 OSC Report, *supra*, n. 269, pp. 24–14. The Ontario Securities Commission has clearly indicated that it does not have to consider the "four pillars" theory since the Ontario government has already given the Dupré Commission the specific mandate of re-examining this question (ibid., pp. 13, 15, 39, 62 and 63; see also *supra*, n. 218).

278. Ibid., pp. iii–v, 26–32, 40–44 and 49–52.

279. Ibid., pp. 27, 28 and 44–49. A brokerage firm whose vested interests had historically been recognized would be required to register as a "foreign dealer registrant." However, such firms would not have to respect the proposed limit of 1.5 percent of their capitalization on the industry as a whole, the Ontario Securities Commission being responsible for establishing the ratio in such cases (ibid., p. 30). Moreover, a financial institution doing business in Canada cannot own more than 30 percent of a "foreign dealer registrant" (Prudential-Bache Securities Ltd. is exempt from this restriction) (ibid., p. 30).

280. Ibid., pp. 33–35, 52 and 53.

281. Ibid., pp. 35–37. For a summary of the exemptions provided for in the Ontario legislation, see appendix 8 of the 1985 OSC Report.

282. Ibid., p. 36. On the other hand, the existing exemptions for government securities, for guaranteed investment certificates issued by trust companies, and for commercial bills would be maintained (ibid., p. 35). The Securities Commission also clearly stated that it did not question the maintenance of certain particular categories of registration such as the "order execution access dealer" (*supra*, nn. 147, 149 and 234) or "type II" registration available to banks for the purchase of their own securities or for other specific operations (ibid., pp. 55, 56 and appendix 8).

283. Ibid., pp. 37, 57 and 58. Contrary to its recommendation on this point in its 1982 report on institutional ownership and diversification of operations (*supra*, n. 275), the Securities Commission concludes that "approval by SROs (self-regulating organizations) of networking proposals would not be required, although the director would generally consult with the SROs on each networking proposal" (ibid., p. 37).

284. Quebec Securities Commission, Decision 6861, *supra*, n. 272, pp. 2.1.1–2.1.4 and 2.1.16–2.1.21. See also the terms and conditions set by the Quebec Securities Com-

mission at p. 2.1.18 as well as the order with respect to the Montreal Stock Exchange at pp. 2.1.20 and 2.1.21, *Securities Act*, S.Q. 1982, c. 48, R.S.Q., c. V-1.1, s. 159; "Règlement sur les valeurs mobilières" (1983), 115 *Gazette officielle du Québec*, p. 1511, order 660-83, s. 228). The overlapping between insurance companies and investment firms has increased in Quebec; see Hugh Anderson, "The Lures of Getting Married," *The Gazette* (Montreal), March 27, 1984, p. C-1. It should be noted that the Quebec Securities Commission requires that at least 40 percent of the board of directors of a brokerage firm be members (Quebec Securities Commission, *Instruction générale* Q-9, s. 9 et seq.).

285. See Alan D. Gray, "Caisses Pops Challenge the Chartered Banks," *Financial Times* (Toronto), September 17, 1983, pp. 11 and 12. Quebec Securities Commission, "Dispense d'inscription à titre de courtier, en vertu de l'article 263 de la Loi, des caisses populaires et d'économie Desjardins de diffuser à l'intérieur de leurs établissements de la publicité sur certains services offerts par la Fiducie à titre de courtier d'exercice restreint, decision 7171" (1984), 15 *Québec Bulletin* 37 (September 14), pp. 2.1.1 et seq. See also Quebec Securities Commission, "Inscription de (Fiducie du Québec) à titre de courtier en valeurs d'exercice restreint, decision 84-E-1176" (1984), 15 *Québec Bulletin* 37 (September 14), pp. 7.1.1 et seq.

286. Angela Barnes, "Takeover of Trust Companies May Delay Credit Union Act," *Globe and Mail* (Toronto), March 5, 1983.

287. Economic Council of Canada, *supra*, n. 202, p. 63; see Royal Bank of Canada, *supra*, n. 276, pp. 11–13.

288. Economic Council of Canada, *supra*, n. 202, pp. 63–65; Dimma, *supra*, n. 217, p. 19; Lortie, *supra*, n. 220, p. 14.

289. Courchene, *supra*, n. 229, c. 5, p. 33.

290. Quebec, Assemblée nationale, *Journal des débats*, June 7, 1984, p. 6797.

291. See green paper, *supra*, n. 220, pp. 2–6.

292. Chant and Dean, *supra*, n. 205, p. 733–35. Canadian Life and Health Insurance Association, *Transcripts* of the Royal Commission on the Economic Union and Development Prospects for Canada, s. 57, Toronto, December 2, 1983, pp. 12098 and 12099 (remarks of Jean-Denis Vincent, president of Alliance compagnie mutuelle d'assurance-vie).

293. Yvon Valcin, *Création d'un centre de recherche et d'information sur la monétique*, submission no. 370 to the Royal Commission on the Economic Union and Development Prospects for Canada, p. 3; Yvon Valcin, "La banque électronique aurait-elle un visage humain?" *Le Devoir*, July 20, 1984, p. 7; Richard Skinulis, "A Free-for-all in ATMs?" *Financial Times* (Toronto), September 10, 1984, p. 13.

The Government of Canada and the governments of some provinces are seriously considering the possibility of paying social security benefits and their employees' salaries electronically. It is predicted that this system will be operational within five years (Canadian Banker's Association, *Transcripts* from the Royal Commission on the Economic Union and Development Prospects for Canada, vol. 56, Toronto, December 2, 1983, pp. 11908–11910). Large corporations, open and closed, are both canvassed for financial contributions with respect to the direct deposit of employees' salaries.

294. *Banks and Banking Law Revision Act, 1980, S.C. 1980–81*, c. 40, s. 58; see Canadian Banker's Association, *supra*, n. 293, p. 11909.

295. Paul Brace, "Electronic Funds Transfer System: Legal Perspectives" (1976), 4 *Osgoode Hall L. J.* 787; Jordan, *supra*, n. 39; Welling, *supra*, n. 22; Howard Eddy, Vers un système de paiements électroniques (Ottawa: Department of Finance and Communications, 1974); Goldstein, *supra*, n. 111; Bradley Crawford, "Does Canada Need a Payment Code?" (1982–1983), 7 *Can. Bus. L. J.* 44; Law Reform Commission of Canada, *Droit commercial: les paiements par virement de crédit* (Ottawa: The Commission, 1978). Nicole l'Heureux, "Les effets de la technologie et la protection des droits des consommateurs dans le paiement bancaire" (1983), 24 *Cahiers de droit* 253.

296. *Bank of Canada Act*, R.S.C. 1970, c. B-2; *Bills of Exchange Act*, R.S.C. 1970, c. B-5

(this act applies only to the transfer of funds in writing); *Canadian Payments Association Act*, S.C. 1980–1981, c. 40. The status of members is limited to federal and provincial deposit institutions only. This restriction makes some other financial intermediaries fear that they will not derive equal benefit from the technological developments which their competitors' diversification depends upon (Association of Financial Corporations, *supra*, n. 163, point C.8.4.; ibid., Transcripts of the Royal Commission on the Economic Union and Development Prospects for Canada, vol. 57, Toronto, December 2, 1983, pp. 12042 and 12043).

297. *Electronic Fund Transfer Act*, Publ. L. no. 95-630, 92 Stat. 3741 (1978) (codified at 15 U.S.C. 1982 ed., c. (41)(vi), p. 1693. See Norman Penney and Donald I. Baker, *The Law of Electronic Fund Transfer Systems* (Boston: Warren, Gordham and Lamont, 1980); L'Heureux, *supra*, n. 295, pp. 276 and 277; Crawford, "New Law to Govern E.F.T.S.?" (1980–1981), 5 *Can. Bus. L. J.* 37, 45. See also the series of articles published by J.F. Crean with respect to the situation in Canada: "Automation and Canadian Banking" (1978), 85 *Canadian Banker and ICB Review* 4, p. 16 et seq.; "The Canadian Payments System" (1978), 85 *Canadian Banker and ICB Review* 5, p. 22 et seq.; "EFTS and the Canadian Payments System" (1978), 85 *Canadian Banker and ICB Review* 6, p. 18 et seq.; "Contrasts in National Payments Systems" (1979), 86 *Canadian Banker and ICB Review* 1, p. 18 et seq.; "Governments, EFTS and the Public Interest" (1979), 86 *Canadian Banker and ICB Review* 2, p. 10 et seq.; "Government, the Bank Act and Reform of the Payment System" (1979), 86 *Canadian Banker and ICB Review* 3, p. 4 et seq.

298. L'Heureux, *supra*, n. 295, pp. 277 and 278; Law Reform Commission, *supra*, n. 295, p. 15 (consent to automation), pp. 82–88 (effect of receipt of a credit transfer) and pp. 88–97 (some aspects of the deposit institution's right to compensation from its clients' accounts).

299. Anisman, *supra*, n. 50, pp. 346–51.

300. Canada, Special Joint Committee of the Senate and the House of Commons, *Constitution of Canada*, Ottawa, 1972, p. 88.

301. Canadian Bar Association, *supra*, n. 2, pp. 110–12.

302. Williamson, *supra*, n. 232, p. 912; see E. Bower Carty, "Effet de la croissance des régimes de pensions d'employeurs sur le marché canadien des actions," in Canada, Task Force on Retirement Income Policy, *The Retirement Income System in Canada: Problems and Alternative Policies for Reform* (Ottawa: Minister of Supply and Services Canada, 1980), vol. 2, appendix 14; Brent King, "Pension Funds Getting Bigger All the Time," *Financial Post 500*, Summer 1984, p. 205 et seq. In the United States, a recent poll (fall of 1984) evaluated at only approximately 10 percent the volume of "big board" transactions carried out by individuals; see Michael Blumstein, "How the Institutions Rule the Market," *New York Times*, November 25, 1984, s. 3, pp. 1 and 21.

303. Business Committee on Pension Policy, *Capital Markets Study*, September 1983, p. Sum 1.

304. See Yves Guérard, "Évolution et perspectives futures" in *La Caisse de dépôt et placement du Québec* (Montreal: C.D. Howe Institute, 1984), p. 41. In 1977, some 49 pension funds held approximately two-thirds of the assets of all plans administered in trust (almost $18 billion dollars). Economic Council of Canada, *supra*, n. 202; Alberta Heritage Savings Trust Fund, *Annual Report, 1982–83*, p. 27; Caisse de dépôt et placement du Québec, *États financiers et statistiques financières — rapport de gestion 83* (Montreal, 1983), p. 49 et seq.).

305. Williamson, *supra*, n. 232, pp. 917–27.

306. Business Committee on Pension Policy, *supra*, n. 303, p. Sum 5, Sum 6 and 65.

307. See Economic Council of Canada, *supra*, n. 125, pp. 59–62, 67 and 69.

308. Canada, Senate, Standing Committee on Legal and Constitutional Affairs, *Proceedings* (testimony of Pierre Lortie, Chairman of the Montreal Stock Exchange with respect to the content of Bill S-31) November 30, 1982, pp. 31:13 and 31:14.

309. Ibid., pp. 31:11, 31:24 and 31A:8, appendix 31-A entitled "Les quinze plus grandes entreprises canadiennes indépendantes."

310. Ibid., p. 31:6.

311. Canadian Life and Health Insurance Association, *supra*, n. 131, pp. 21 and 22; Confédération des caisses populaires et d'économie Desjardins, *Submission to the Royal Commission on the Economic Union and Development Prospects for Canada*, submission no. 629, 1983, p. 26.

312. *Act respecting the Caisse de dépôt et placement du Québec*, R.S.Q., c. L-2, ss. 8 and 32. Claude Forget "Introduction sommaire des conclusions," in *La Caisse de dépôt et placement du Québec* (Montreal: C.D. Howe Institute, 1984), pp. 11 and 12.

313. See *Alberta Heritage Savings Trust Fund Act*, R.S.Q. 1980, c. A-27 as amended. The fund is divided into five divisions: Capital Projects Division, Canada Investment Division, Alberta Investment Division, Energy Investment Division and Commercial Investment Division; see, generally, on this subject, Alan A. Warrack, "Making Sense of the Alberta Heritage Fund (1983), 48 *Business Quarterly* 2, pp. 23–27; and the special issue of the journal, *Canadian Public Policy*, which is devoted to the subject of the fund ("The Alberta Heritage Savings Trust Fund" (1980), 6 *Canadian Public Policy* 141, pp. 141–280); Alberta Heritage Savings Trust Fund, *Annual Report 1982–1983*.

314. See Thomas J. Courchene and James R. Melvin, "Energy Revenues: Consequences for the Rest of Canada" (1980), 6 *Canadian Public Policy* 192, at p. 203.

315. Economic Council of Canada, *supra*, n. 202, pp. 52 and 60; Canada Deposit Insurance Corporation, *Annual Report: Year Ended December 31, 1982*, p. 16.

316. See Ontario, Ministry of Consumer and Commercial Relations, *Special Report of the Registrar Concerning Crown Trust Company, Greymac Trust Company, Seaway Trust Company, Greymac Mortgage Corporation and Seaway Mortgage Corporation* (Toronto, November 1983), pp. 8, 9 and 12–14; Canada Deposit Insurance Corporation, *supra*, n. 315, and *Annual Report — Year Ended December 31, 1983*, Arthur Johnson, "Watchdog Cites Gap in Dealing with Trust Firms," *Globe and Mail* September 28, 1983, p. RB-1.

The losses assumed by the Canada Deposit Insurance Corporation were, however, considerable, the Canada Deposit Insurance Corporation itself facing a deficit of some $650 million as a result of loans granted to eight member institutions (see Canadian Banker's Association, *Comments on Deposit Insurance Reform*, Ottawa, November 1984, p. 11).

317. *Canada Deposit Insurance Corporation Act*, R.S.C. 1970, c. C-3, section 13(1)(c), as amended by S.C. 1983, c. 142, s. 3. In fact, the protection provided by the Canada Deposit Insurance Corporation exceeds the theoretical limit of $60,000, since the procedure, followed since 1982, to entrust to a third party the management of an institution in difficulty, rather than liquidating it, is equivalent to complete protection of insured and uninsured depositors as well as non-guaranteed creditors (Canadian Banker's Association, *supra*, n. 308, pp. 5, 6, 11 et seq., and appendixes C and E. The federal Minister of State for Finance, Barbara McDougall, has also set up a task force to review the deposit insurance scheme.

318. Confédération des caisses populaires et d'économie Desjardins du Québec, *supra*, n. 303, p. 27; see also Dimma, *supra*, n. 265, p. 20; Canadian Banker's Association, *supra*, n. 263, pp. 15 and 16; and *supra*, n. 316, p. 10.

319. Economic Council of Canada, *supra*, n. 202, p. 60; any provincial institution which is a member of the Canada Deposit Insurance Corporation must, by the terms of the *Canada Deposit Insurance Corporation Act*, R.S.C. c. C-3, as amended, agree "in carrying on its business, not to exercise powers substantially different" from those which a federal trust or loan company could exercise [ibid., s. 16(b)]. The Comité québécois d'étude des institutions financières noted that the scope of s. 16(b) is such that it "abolishes, for all practical purposes, the control which a provincial charter can give to the Government of Quebec over all institutions which are insured by virtue of the *Deposit Insurance Act*" (Comité d'études sur les institutions financières, *supra*, n. 21, p. 134). The federal act was to be amended in order to make way for specific agreements between the Canada Deposit Insurance Corporation and a province (ibid., s. 31–33). Such an agreement does exist in the case of Quebec.

320. *Banks and Banking Law Revision Act, 1980*, S.C. 1980–81, c. 40, part IV; *Canadian Payments Association Act*, s. 84; Règlement de compensation de l'Association canadienne des paiements (1983), 117 *Gazette du Canada* 494, s. 17, p. 505.

321. With respect to the powers of corporations, see Stanley M. Beck, "Corporate Power and Public Policy" in *Consumer Protection, Environmental Law and Corporate Power*, volume 50 of the research studies prepared for the Royal Commission on the Economic Union and Development Prospects for Canada (Toronto: University of Toronto Press, 1985). See also I.A. Litvak and C.J. Maule, *The Canadian Multinationals* (Toronto: Butterworth, 1981); R.T. Naylor, *The History of Canadian Business, 1867–1914* (Toronto: James Lorimer, 1975); Jorge Niosi, *Canadian Capitalism: A Study of Power in the Canadian Business Establishment* (Toronto: James Lorimer, 1981); Walter Stewart, *The Canadian Banks: Towers of Gold — Feet of Clay* (Toronto: Totem, 1983); W. Clement, *The Canadian Corporate Elite* (Toronto: McClelland and Stewart, 1975); Jean-Guy Loranger, *Le Capital financier au Canada, illusion ou réalité?* (Paris: cahiers du CPREMAP, 1979); François Moreau, *Le Capital financier québécois* (Quebec: Éditions coopératives Alberta Saint-Martine, Centrale de l'enseignement du Québec, 1981); Rod McQueen, *The Money-Spinners* (Toronto: Macmillan, 1983). The Bryce Commission was very sceptical about the significance of the influence of large corporations on government policy, Canada, *Report* (Ottawa: Royal Commission on Corporate Concentration, Minister of Supply and Services Canada, 1978).

322. See, by way of example, the case of the Campeau Corporation's attempt to control Royal Trustco, McQueen, *supra*, n. 321, pp. 49–52; John L. Howard, "Sparling v. Royal Trustco: The Representative Role of the Director Under the CBCA" (1985), 10 *Can. Bus. L. J.* 35.

323. Canada, Royal Commission on Bilingualism and Biculturalism, *Report*, book 3, *The Work World* (Ottawa: Queen's Printer, 1969); and *Preliminary Report* (Ottawa: Queen's Printer, 1965), pp. 68–73.

324. Canada, Comité d'étude sur les institutions financières, *supra*, n. 21, pp. 227 and 288.

325. André Rybe, "Le secteur financier et le dévelopement économique du Québec" (1974), 50 *Actualité économique* 379.

326. Pierre Lortie, *Raising Public Equity Capital in Canada — The Montreal Exchange: An Important Factor in the Overall Equation*, speech delivered at the 66th annual meeting of the Canadian Bar Association, Winnipeg, August 28, 1984; Pierre Lortie, *Le financement public des entreprises: un bilan préliminaire* (Montreal: Montreal Stock Exchange, September 4, 1984); *La Capitalisation des entreprises au Québec — rapport au ministre de l'Industrie, du Commerce et du Tourisme du Québec*, June 1984 (commonly called the Saucier Report from the name of its chairman, Serge Saucier, chairman and chief executive officer of Raymond, Chabot, Martine, Paré and Assoc.); Christiane Langevin, *L'industrie québécoise du financement public: une analyse structurelle*, rapport présenté à la Commission québécoise sur la capitalisation des entreprises, Montreal, Secor Inc., June 1984; "La Bourse de Montréal," *Le Devoir*, September 14, 1984, cahier 3; Marie-Agnès Thellier, "Le projet de loi 75 pourra générer une explosion des affaires pour les institutions québécoises," *Le Devoir*, April 21, 1984, p. 15; Jacques McNish, "Insurance Firms Anxious to Push into Quebec," *Financial Times* (Toronto), July 7, 1984, p. 3; Amy Booth, "Laurentian Group to Leap Financial Barriers," *Financial Post* (Toronto), July 7, 1984, pp. 1 and 2.

327. Moreau, *supra*, n. 321, p. 55–113; Michel Nadeau, "La concentration de l'épargne," *Le Devoir*, November 17, 1982.

328. The Laurentian Group, *La Synergie canadienne*, submission no. 493 to the Royal Commission on the Economic Union and Development Prospects for Canada, November 1983, p. 7; see also the testimony of Claude Castonguay, chairman and chief executive officer of the Laurentian Group Corporation before the Commission, in Montreal, November 2, 1983, *Transcripts*, volume 39, pp. 7739–41. See also, Alain Dubuc, "La Caisse de dépôt victime de chauvinisme ontarien," *La Presse*, January 21, 1982.
    As another example of the cultural tensions between the French-speaking and the

English-speaking business communities, see Eric Starkman, "P.Q. Propping Up Montreal Exchange for Political Reasons: TSE President," *The Gazette*, October 22, 1984, p. A-9.

329. In the press, see Alain Dubuc, "S-31 à la poubelle," *La Presse*, November 24, 1983, p. C-1; Raymond Giroux, "Mulroney à l'aide du Québec," *Le Soleil* (Quebec), November 22, 1983, p. A-14; Jean-Claude Leclerc, "Un coup opportun," *Le Devoir*, November 22, 1983, p. 6; Jean-Paul Gagné, "S-31: rien de changé malgré le maquillage," *Les Affaires* (Montreal), November 12, 1983, p. 6; Jacques Dumas, "Ottawa réédite la même bêtise," *Le Soleil* (Quebec), November 9, 1983, p. A-14; Michel Nadeau, "L'obsession au S-31," *Le Devoir*, November 8, 1983, p. 12; Armand Sales, "Le Canadien Pacifique à l'abri sous le S-31," *Le Devoir*, November 8, 1983, p. 13; Michel Nadeau, "Le bon sens des sénateurs," *Le Devoir*, December 18, 1982; Michel Roy, "L'opération ratée du Cabinet fédéral," *La Presse*, December 9, 1982; Marcel Pépin, "Arguments incomplets de Trudeau," *Le Soleil* (Quebec), December 3, 1982; Michel Nadeau, "Une loi pour CP et Alcan," *Le Devoir*, December 2, 1982; Ivan Guay, "Le projet de loi S-31 est le pire des trompe-l'oeil," *La Presse*, November 29, 1982; Michel Roy, "Laisser mourir le projet de loi S-31," *La Presse*, November 27, 1982; Pierre Bergeron, "Un bien drôle de projet de loi," *Le Droit* (Ottawa), November 15, 1982; Lise Bissonnette, "Un coup impérial," *Le Devoir*, November 5, 1982; and Jean-Guy Dubuc, "Étrange contrôle sur le transport," *La Presse*, November 5, 1982.

For the business world, see Canada, Senate, Standing Committee on Legal and Constitutional Affairs, *Proceedings* (testimony of the chairman, Serge Saucier, and of the vice-president and general manager, André Vallerand, of the Montreal Chamber of Commerce) December 7, 1982, pp. 34:7–34:37; and ibid., *Deliberations*, (testimony of Pierre Lortie, chairman of the Montreal Stock Exchange), November 30, 1982.

There is an analysis of the debate over the tabling and the ultimate abandonment of Bill S-31 on the House of Commons order paper in Allan Tupper, *Bill S-31 and the Federalism of State Capitalism*, document no. 18 (Kingston: Queen's University, Institute for Intergovernmental Relations, August 1983).

330. Canada, Comité d'étude sur les institutions financières, *supra*, n. 21, pp. 227–39; Tetley Report, *supra*, n. 132; Quebec, Ministry of Economic Development, *L'épargne — rapport du groupe de travail sur l'épargne au Québec* (Quebec: Éditeur officiel du Québec, 1980), pp. 542 and 543.

331. *An Act respecting the Caisse de dépôt et placement du Québec*, S.Q. 1965, c. 23, R.S.Q., c. C-2; see D.H. Fullerton, "La Caisse de dépôt — un retour en arrière" in *La Caisse de dépôt et placement du Québec* (Montreal: C.D. Howe Institute, 1984), pp. 24–27; Heward Graftey, "Government and Business: The Caisse de dépôt et placement du Québec — Understanding the Quebec Background" (1983), 48 *Business Quarterly*, special supplement (July 1982), p. 19; Moreau, *supra*, n. 313, pp. 55–59.

332. Canada, Comité d'étude sur les institutions financières, *supra*, n. 21, pp. 234 and 235; Quebec, Ministry of Economic Development, *supra*, no. 330, pp. 617–28.

333. Marcel Coté and Jean Coursielle, "La perception de la Caisse de dépôt et placement du Québec par les chefs d'entreprises," in *La Caisse de dépôt et placement du Québec* (Montreal: C.D. Howe Institute, 1984), pp. 74–83.

334. Claude Forget, "Introduction et sommaire des conclusions" in *La Caisse de dépôt et placement du Québec* (Montreal: C.D. Howe Institute, 1984), pp. 13–15; François Roberge, "La Caisse de dépôt n'a gagné qu'une prise," *Finance* (Montreal), December 5, 1983, pp. 2 and 3.

335. La Caisse de dépôt et placement, "Le conseil du patront est déçu de la réaction du ministre des finances," *Journal de Québec* (Quebec), April 14, 1983; "Government's Caisse Urged to Limit Investments," *The Gazette* (Montreal), August 24, 1984, p. B-6.

336. See John N. Benson, *Provincial Government Banks: A Case Study of Regional Response to National Institutions* (Vancouver: Fraser Institute, 1978), pp. 9–36.

337. See the speech of the Committee of the Premiers of Manitoba, Alberta, Saskatchewan and British Columbia, *Capital Financing and Regional Financial Institutions*, Con-

ference on Economic Prospects for Western Canada, Calgary, July 24–26, 1973; Canada, *Capital Financing and Regional Financial Institutions*, document prepared for the 1973 Conference on Economic Prospects for the West, Calgary, July 24–26, 1973; "The Banks and the West: Facts, Figures and the Future" (1973), 16 *Canadian Bankers Association Bulletin*, Benson, *supra*, n. 336, p. 19.

338. *Banks and Banking Law Revision Act, 1980*, S.C. 1980–81, c. 40, s. 114. See Canada, Department of Finance, *supra*, n. 4, p. 23; Canada, Senate, *supra*, n. 214, p. 44:41; Canada, Senate, *supra*, n. 232, pp. 30:103 and 30:104; Canada, Senate, Senate Standing Committee on Banking, Trade and Commerce, *Report on the Content of Bill C-14*, December 4, 1979, pp. 12:9 and 12:20.

339. Alberta, *White Paper — Proposals for an Industrial and Science Strategy for Albertans — 1985 to 1990*, Edmonton, July 1984, p. 42. See also *Excerpts of Premier Peter Lougheed's Speech to the Edmonton Chamber of Commerce*, Edmonton, July 11, 1984.

340. Ibid., p. 50. See Jane Becker, "Banker Suggests Alberta Sell Treasury Branch Operations," *Globe and Mail*, September 27, 1984, p. RB-6.

341. Garth Stevenson, "Political Constraints and the Province Building Objective" (1980), 6 *Canadian Public Policy* 265, at pp. 268–71.

342. Alberta, *supra*, n. 339, pp. 45 and 64.

343. See Alberta Heritage Savings Trust Fund, *Annual Report 1982–83*, p. 7; and Lou Hyndman, *1984 Budget Address*, March 27, 1984, p. 32 et seq.

344. S.B.C. 1975, c. 68.

345. E.R. Black and A.C. Cairns, "A Different Perspective on Canadian Federalism" in J.P. Meekison (ed.), *Canadian Federalism: Myth or Reality* (Toronto: Methuen, 1966), pp. 81–97; Stevenson, *supra*, n. 341, pp. 265–74.

346. Canadian Bar Association, *supra*, n. 2, pp. 95–100.

347. Canada, Task Force on Canadian Unity, *A Future Together* (Ottawa: Minister of Supply and Services Canada, 1979), p. 124, recommendation 23.

348. Ontario Advisory Committee on Confederation, *Second Report: The Federal–Provincial Distribution of Powers* (Toronto: The Committee, 1979), pp. 14–16; Ontario, Select Committee on Constitutional Reform, *Report* (Toronto: October 1980), p. 18; Statement by the Premier of Ontario, William G. Davis, "Power Sharing," document 800-8-049, p. 14 in *Federal-Provincial Conference of First Ministers*, Ottawa, October 31, 1978 (Ottawa: Canadian Intergovernmental Conference Secretariat, 1978).

349. Quebec, Conseil exécutif, *La nouvelle entente Quebec–Canada* (Quebec: Éditeur officiel du Québec, 1980), p. 63.

350. Quebec Liberal Party, Constitutional Committee, *Une nouvelle fédération canadienne*, [s.1] [s.éd.], 1980, pp. 109–112, Quebec Liberal Party, *supra*, n. 5, pp. 18–20.

351. Canada, *Economic Powers*, *supra*, n. 17; Canada, *Powers over the Economy: Constitutional Basis of the Canadian Economic Union*, document 830-81-036 in *Meeting of the Continuing Committee of Ministers on the Constitution*, Montreal, July 9, 1980, (Ottawa: Canadian Intergovernmental Conference Secretariat, 1980). Let us remember that, at the time of the First Ministers' Conference on the Constitution held in January 1979, the federal government had demonstrated its desire to tackle "the issue of non-tariff barriers with respect to commerce and investment on an international and interprovincial scale." Canada, *"Deuxieme liste" d'articles à l'étude pour la suite de la révision constitutionnelle*, document 800-10/026 in *Federal-Provincial First Ministers' Conference on the Constitution*, Ottawa, February 5 and 6, 1979 (Ottawa: Canadian Intergovernmental Conference Secretariat, 1979).

352. Chrétien, *supra*, n. 2, pp. 2, 20, 30, 44 and 45. The text of the federal document states: "Consequently, provincial legislation and regulation must be capable of variation from province to province, and such variation will inevitably cause some impediments to economic mobility, but these must be kept within the bounds of necessity" (ibid., p. 30).

353. Canada, *supra*, n. 17, pp. 2 and 3.

354. Canada, *Powers over the Economy: Options Submitted for Consideration by the Government of Canada to Safeguard the Canadian Economic Union in the Constitution*, document no. 830-82/007 in *Meeting of the Continuing Committee of Ministers on the Constitution* (Ottawa: Canadian Intergovernmental Conference Secretariat, 1980), appendices B and C.

355. Saskatchewan, "The Canadian Economic Union — Draft," document no. 83-83/004 in *Meeting of the Continuing Committee of Ministers on the Constitution* (Ottawa: Canadian Intergovernmental Conference Secretariat, 1980).

356. *Textes légaux formant les annexes des rapports du CPMC aux premiers ministres*, document 800-14/061 in *Federal-Provincial First Ministers' Conference on the Constitution* (Ottawa: Canadian Intergovernmental Conference Secretariat, 1980). See also Canada, *Notes à l'intention de l'honorable William G. Davis, premier ministre de l'Ontario*, document no. 800-14/079 in *First Ministers' Conference on the Constitution* (Ottawa: Canadian Intergovernmental Conference Secretariat, 1980); Saskatchewan, *Powers over the Economy — The Position of Saskatchewan*, document no. 800-14/028 in *Federal-Provincial First Ministers' Conference on the Constitution* (Ottawa: Canadian Intergovernmental Conference Secretariat, 1980).

The "undue manner" test was abandoned because it was not accurate enough (see Federal-Provincial First Ministers' Conference on the Constitution, Ottawa, September 8–13, 1980, *Verbatim Transcript* (Ottawa: Canadian Intergovernmental Conference Secretariat, 1980), p. 803 (see also the remarks of the Quebec Minister of Finance, Jacques Parizeau, pp. 786 and 787). See, generally, Roy Romanow, John Whyte and Howard Leeson, *Canada Notwithstanding* (Toronto: Carswell/Methuen, 1984), pp. 92 and 93.

357. Saskatchewan, *Powers over the Economy — Analysis of Federal Proposals*, document no. 800-14/029 in *Federal-Provincial First Ministers' Conference on the Constitution* (Ottawa: Canadian Intergovernmental Conference Secretariat, 1980), pp. 12 and 13; see, Federal-Provincial Conference, *supra*, n. 356, p. 849.

358. *Federal-Provincial Conference, supra*, n. 356, p. 366 (Manitoba), pp. 778–92 and 871–76 (Quebec), pp. 808–19 (British Columbia), pp. 793–800 (New Brunswick), pp. 848–58 (Saskatchewan), pp. 827 and 828 (Alberta), p. 847 (Newfoundland), pp. 829–36 (Nova Scotia), pp. 772–77 and 855–77 (Ontario).

359. Saskatchewan, *supra*, n. 356, pp. 2, 4 and 5. Saskatchewan, *Analysis of Federal Proposals, supra*, n. 357, p. 12; and Allan Blakeney, *Opening Speech — Powers over the Economy*, document no 800-14/025 in *Federal-Provincial First Ministers' Conference on the Constitution* (Ottawa: Canadian Intergovernmental Conference Secretariat, 1980).

In order to gain a better understanding of the importance of government support of the private sector (in the form of loans or financial guarantees), it should be noted that in 1980 the Economic Council of Canada listed 28 federal or provincial agencies whose primary activity consisted of offering such services (Economic Council of Canada, *supra*, n. 8, p. 17 et seq.).

360. Royal Commission on the Economic Union and Development Prospects for Canada, *A Commission on the Future of Canada — Challenges and Choices* (Ottawa: Minister of Supply and Services Canada, 1984), p. 66.

361. A comparative study of the constitutional mechanisms for maintaining and promoting the American economic union is given in Bernier, et al., *supra*, n. 3.

362. A comparative study of the constitutional mechanisms for maintaining and promoting the Australian economic union is given in Bernier, et al., *supra*, n. 3.

# THE COLLECTED RESEARCH STUDIES

## Royal Commission on the Economic Union and Development Prospects for Canada

### ECONOMICS

**Income Distribution and Economic Security in Canada** (Vol. 1), *François Vaillancourt, Research Coordinator*

Vol. 1   Income Distribution and Economic Security in Canada, *F. Vaillancourt* (C)*

**Industrial Structure** (Vols. 2-8), *Donald G. McFetridge, Research Coordinator*

Vol. 2   Canadian Industry in Transition, *D.G. McFetridge* (C)
Vol. 3   Technological Change in Canadian Industry, *D.G. McFetridge* (C)
Vol. 4   Canadian Industrial Policy in Action, *D.G. McFetridge* (C)
Vol. 5   Economics of Industrial Policy and Strategy, *D.G. McFetridge* (C)
Vol. 6   The Role of Scale in Canada–US Productivity Differences, *J.R. Baldwin and P.K. Gorecki* (M)
Vol. 7   Competition Policy and Vertical Exchange, *F. Mathewson and R. Winter* (M)
Vol. 8   The Political Economy of Economic Adjustment, *M. Trebilcock* (M)

**International Trade** (Vols. 9-14), *John Whalley, Research Coordinator*

Vol. 9   Canadian Trade Policies and the World Economy, *J. Whalley with C. Hamilton and R. Hill* (M)
Vol. 10   Canada and the Multilateral Trading System, *J. Whalley* (M)
Vol. 11   Canada–United States Free Trade, *J. Whalley* (C)
Vol. 12   Domestic Policies and the International Economic Environment, *J. Whalley* (C)
Vol. 13   Trade, Industrial Policy and International Competition, *R. Harris* (M)
Vol. 14   Canada's Resource Industries and Water Export Policy, *J. Whalley* (C)

**Labour Markets and Labour Relations** (Vols. 15-18), *Craig Riddell, Research Coordinator*

Vol. 15   Labour-Management Cooperation in Canada, *C. Riddell* (C)
Vol. 16   Canadian Labour Relations, *C. Riddell* (C)
Vol. 17   Work and Pay: The Canadian Labour Market, *C. Riddell* (C)
Vol. 18   Adapting to Change: Labour Market Adjustment in Canada, *C. Riddell* (C)

**Macroeconomics** (Vols. 19-25), *John Sargent, Research Coordinator*

Vol. 19   Macroeconomic Performance and Policy Issues: Overviews, *J. Sargent* (M)
Vol. 20   Post-War Macroeconomic Developments, *J. Sargent* (C)
Vol. 21   Fiscal and Monetary Policy, *J. Sargent* (C)
Vol. 22   Economic Growth: Prospects and Determinants, *J. Sargent* (C)
Vol. 23   Long-Term Economic Prospects for Canada: A Symposium, *J. Sargent* (C)
Vol. 24   Foreign Macroeconomic Experience: A Symposium, *J. Sargent* (C)
Vol. 25   Dealing with Inflation and Unemployment in Canada, *C. Riddell* (M)

**Economic Ideas and Social Issues** (Vols. 26 and 27), *David Laidler, Research Coordinator*

Vol. 26   Approaches to Economic Well-Being, *D. Laidler* (C)
Vol. 27   Responses to Economic Change, *D. Laidler* (C)

* (C) denotes a Collection of studies by various authors coordinated by the person named.
  (M) denotes a Monograph.

## POLITICS AND INSTITUTIONS OF GOVERNMENT

**Canada and the International Political Economy** (Vols. 28-30), *Denis Stairs and Gilbert R. Winham, Research Coordinators*

Vol. 28 Canada and the International Political/Economic Environment, *D. Stairs and G.R. Winham* (C)
Vol. 29 The Politics of Canada's Economic Relationship with the United States, *D. Stairs and G.R. Winham* (C)
Vol. 30 Selected Problems in Formulating Foreign Economic Policy, *D. Stairs and G.R. Winham* (C)

**State and Society in the Modern Era** (Vols. 31 and 32), *Keith Banting, Research Coordinator*

Vol. 31 State and Society: Canada in Comparative Perspective, *K. Banting* (C)
Vol. 32 The State and Economic Interests, *K. Banting* (C)

**Constitutionalism, Citizenship and Society** (Vols. 33-35), *Alan Cairns and Cynthia Williams, Research Coordinators*

Vol. 33 Constitutionalism, Citizenship and Society in Canada, *A. Cairns and C. Williams* (C)
Vol. 34 The Politics of Gender, Ethnicity and Language in Canada, *A. Cairns and C. Williams* (C)
Vol. 35 Public Opinion and Public Policy in Canada, *R. Johnston* (M)

**Representative Institutions** (Vols. 36-39), *Peter Aucoin, Research Coordinator*

Vol. 36 Party Government and Regional Representation in Canada, *P. Aucoin* (C)
Vol. 37 Regional Responsiveness and the National Administrative State, *P. Aucoin* (C)
Vol. 38 Institutional Reforms for Representative Government, *P. Aucoin* (C)
Vol. 39 Intrastate Federalism in Canada, *D.V. Smiley and R.L. Watts* (M)

**The Politics of Economic Policy** (Vols. 40-43), *G. Bruce Doern, Research Coordinator*

Vol. 40 The Politics of Economic Policy, *G.B. Doern* (C)
Vol. 41 Federal and Provincial Budgeting, *A.M. Maslove, M.J. Prince and G.B. Doern* (M)
Vol. 42 Economic Regulation and the Federal System, *R. Schultz and A. Alexandroff* (M)
Vol. 43 Bureaucracy in Canada: Control and Reform, *S.L. Sutherland and G.B. Doern* (M)

**Industrial Policy** (Vols. 44 and 45), *André Blais, Research Coordinator*

Vol. 44 Industrial Policy, *A. Blais* (C)
Vol. 45 The Political Sociology of Industrial Policy, *A. Blais* (M)

## LAW AND CONSTITUTIONAL ISSUES

**Law, Society and the Economy** (Vols. 46-51), *Ivan Bernier and Andrée Lajoie, Research Coordinators*

Vol. 46 Law, Society and the Economy, *I. Bernier and A. Lajoie* (C)
Vol. 47 The Supreme Court of Canada as an Instrument of Political Change, *I. Bernier and A. Lajoie* (C)
Vol. 48 Regulations, Crown Corporations and Administrative Tribunals, *I. Bernier and A. Lajoie* (C)
Vol. 49 Family Law and Social Welfare Legislation in Canada, *I. Bernier and A. Lajoie* (C)
Vol. 50 Consumer Protection, Environmental Law and Corporate Power, *I. Bernier and A. Lajoie* (C)
Vol. 51 Labour Law and Urban Law in Canada, *I. Bernier and A. Lajoie* (C)

**The International Legal Environment** (Vols. 52-54), *John Quinn, Research Coordinator*

Vol. 52 The International Legal Environment, *J. Quinn* (C)
Vol. 53 Canadian Economic Development and the International Trading System, *M.M. Hart* (M)
Vol. 54 Canada and the New International Law of the Sea, *D.M. Johnston* (M)

**Harmonization of Laws in Canada** (Vols. 55 and 56), *Ronald C.C. Cuming, Research Coordinator*

Vol. 55 Perspectives on the Harmonization of Law in Canada, *R. Cuming* (C)
Vol. 56 Harmonization of Business Law in Canada, *R. Cuming* (C)

**Institutional and Constitutional Arrangements** (Vols. 57 and 58), *Clare F. Beckton and A. Wayne MacKay, Research Coordinators*

Vol. 57 Recurring Issues in Canadian Federalism, *C.F. Beckton and A.W. MacKay* (C)
Vol. 58 The Courts and The Charter, *C.F. Beckton and A.W. MacKay* (C)

## FEDERALISM AND THE ECONOMIC UNION

**Federalism and The Economic Union** (Vols. 58-72), *Mark Krasnick, Kenneth Norrie and Richard Simeon, Research Coordinators*

Vol. 59 Federalism and Economic Union in Canada, *K. Norrie, R. Simeon and M. Krasnick* (M)
Vol. 60 Perspectives on the Canadian Economic Union, *M. Krasnick* (C)
Vol. 61 Division of Powers and Public Policy, *R. Simeon* (C)
Vol. 62 Case Studies in the Division of Powers, *M. Krasnick* (C)
Vol. 63 Intergovernmental Relations, *R. Simeon* (C)
Vol. 64 Disparities and Interregional Adjustment, *K. Norrie* (C)
Vol. 65 Fiscal Federalism, *M. Krasnick* (C)
Vol. 66 Mobility of Capital in the Canadian Economic Union, *N. Roy* (M)
Vol. 67 Economic Management and the Division of Powers, *T.J. Courchene* (M)
Vol. 68 Regional Aspects of Confederation, *J. Whalley* (M)
Vol. 69 Interest Groups in the Canadian Federal System, *H.G. Thorburn* (M)
Vol. 70 Canada and Quebec, Past and Future: An Essay, *D. Latouche* (M)
Vol. 71 The Political Economy of Canadian Federalism: 1940-1984, *R. Simeon and I. Robinson* (M)

## THE NORTH

Vol. 72 The North, *Michael S. Whittington, Coordinator* (C)

# COMMISSION ORGANIZATION

## Chairman
Donald S. Macdonald

## Commissioners

| | | |
|---|---|---|
| Clarence L. Barber | William M. Hamilton | Daryl K. Seaman |
| Albert Breton | John R. Messer | Thomas K. Shoyama |
| M. Angela Cantwell Peters | Laurent Picard | Jean Casselman-Wadds |
| E. Gérard Docquier | Michel Robert | Catherine T. Wallace |

## Senior Officers

*Executive Director*
J. Gerald Godsoe

| *Director of Policy* | *Senior Advisors* | *Directors of Research* |
|---|---|---|
| Alan Nymark | David Ablett | Ivan Bernier |
| | Victor Clarke | Alan Cairns |
| *Secretary* | Carl Goldenberg | David C. Smith |
| Michel Rochon | Harry Stewart | |
| | | |
| *Director of Administration* | *Director of Publishing* | *Co-Directors of Research* |
| Sheila-Marie Cook | Ed Matheson | Kenneth Norrie |
| | | John Sargent |

## Research Program Organization

| Economics | Politics and the Institutions of Government | Law and Constitutional Issues |
|---|---|---|
| *Research Director* | *Research Director* | *Research Director* |
| David C. Smith | Alan Cairns | Ivan Bernier |
| | | |
| *Executive Assistant & Assistant Director (Research Services)* | *Executive Assistant* | *Executive Assistant & Research Program Administrator* |
| I. Lilla Connidis | Karen Jackson | Jacques J.M. Shore |
| | | |
| *Coordinators* | *Coordinators* | *Coordinators* |
| David Laidler | Peter Aucoin | Clare F. Beckton |
| Donald G. McFetridge | Keith Banting | Ronald C.C. Cuming |
| Kenneth Norrie* | André Blais | Mark Krasnick |
| Craig Riddell | Bruce Doern | Andrée Lajoie |
| John Sargent* | Richard Simeon | A. Wayne MacKay |
| François Vaillancourt | Denis Stairs | John J. Quinn |
| John Whalley | Cynthia Williams | |
| | Gilbert R. Winham | |
| | | |
| *Research Analysts* | *Research Analysts* | *Administrative and Research Assistant* |
| Caroline Digby | Claude Desranleau | Nicolas Roy |
| Mireille Ethier | Ian Robinson | |
| Judith Gold | | |
| Douglas S. Green | *Office Administration* | *Research Analyst* |
| Colleen Hamilton | Donna Stebbing | Nola Silzer |
| Roderick Hill | | |
| Joyce Martin | | |

*Kenneth Norrie and John Sargent co-directed the final phase of Economics Research with David Smith